Public Figures, Private Lives:

An Introduction to Protective Security for High Net Worth Individuals and Family Offices

Christian West
Brian Jantzen
Ivor Terret
Jared Van Driessche

edited by
Terry Dunne

Public Figures, Private Lives:

An Introduction to Protective Security for High Net Worth Individuals and

Family Offices

Library of Congress

Cataloging-in-Publication Data

ISBN 978-1-7328021-0-0

Library of Congress Control Number: 2018960035

Published by AS Solution

Bellevue, Washington, USA

An SOS Security Company

Dedication

To all the men and women

who work in the protective security industry

Contents

Introduction: The WHY of family protective security: Safe, happy, productive – and private

We're pleased to present this book and see the results of a project we've been working on for a long time.

We started talking about this project after the publication of *Corporate Executive Protection: An Introduction for Corporations and Security Professionals* in 2016. In that, AS Solution's first book, Christian and Brian examined some of the key questions that people new to executive protection in corporate contexts often ask. Written for the principals who are the beneficiaries of executive protection, corporate decision makers who are involved in procuring and managing such services, and security practitioners who want to work in the field, the book was a general introduction that attempted to explain why executive protection is relevant to many in the C-suite, how successful programs are built and managed, and what stages corporate executive protection programs typically go through.

We were grateful for the enthusiastic response to our first book, now in its second printing. Our objective was not to write a "how to" book on security tactics, but rather to help readers understand why and how successful corporate programs are built, and to enable them to become better and more critical protectees, protectors, and participants in the mission of keeping people safe, happy and productive in corporate contexts.

This approach seemed to strike a chord with readers of many different backgrounds. But our first book's success also led to many requests for more, something similar, but different: What about security for high net worth individuals and families? Security in corporate contexts, with board-mandated executive protection programs and the involvement of many departmental managers and other stakeholders is one thing. Security in the sanctity of the home, within the privacy boundaries of the family, is something completely different. Could we write on that, too?

Of course, security for high net worth individuals is an important part of what we do, too, and we have a lot of experience – and probably even more opinions – about it. There are many similar reasons for why corporations and families choose professional protection solutions, and there are also many similarities in how programs are designed and run. But there are also many differences. So many, we decided to embark on our second book project, *Public Figures, Private Lives: An Introduction to Protective Security for High Net Worth Individuals and Family Offices.*

To help us expand our perspective, we decided early on to ask Jared and Ivor to join us in writing this new book. We've all worked together for years with both corporate and private clients, and although Ivor and Jared have moved on after stints in AS Solution, both remain close friends and trusted colleagues in the industry.

This book is a collective effort that brings together our shared experience in helping high net worth individuals and families achieve the kind of security that works for them. Like our first book, we focus more on "why" and "what" than the "how-to". We do not believe that anyone can learn how to deliver professional security simply by reading a book. We do believe that anyone concerned with professional security, whether principal or practitioner, can benefit from understanding more about high-performance security services in specific contexts – and be better equipped to ask critical questions.

Readers of our first book will notice a number of similarities between that and this, our second book. We have structured both books in similar ways (and have added a fourth section in this volume); book two repurposes a number of chapters from the corporate context to the private and have been rewritten accordingly; both books contain material previously published on our blog, as well as new material. We begin each of this book's four parts with a story, all of which are based on actual experience but completely anonymized; we hope these anecdotes will help readers on both sides of the protective relationship to understand how some of the topics presented in this book play out in the real world.

Readers are invited to use this book as it best suits their purposes. Some will read only the parts they find most relevant; some will read it from end to end; others might not get past Chapter 1. We encourage you to get an overview of the book by reading the introductions to all of its four parts, then choose where to go from there.

Part I lays out the foundations of family protective security. The first seven chapters are a good place to start if you want to get an overview of why high net worth individuals and families opt for professional security, the basics on how security programs work, the ecosystems in which they take place, as well as chapters on secure travel, intelligence programs, and legal compliance issues.

In Part II, we examine a number of topics pertinent to understanding how family protective programs should be managed. We begin with some thoughts on how to set objectives for family security programs, then dig into a range of personnel and program management issues before closing the section with some advice on the procurement of professional protective services.

Part III deals with transitions in family protective security programs, from startup to turnaround. We also offer some ideas on how to realign a protective program that is seemingly in good shape but actually headed for trouble, as well as a chapter on how to sustain high performance in effective programs. The final chapter in Part III deals with a transition that affects many families, separation and divorce, and some of the challenges this poses for security teams.

Does any family really want anything less than the best available security personnel? Ours is a people business, and the success of our programs depends directly on how successful we are in matching the right people to the right programs. The final section of our book, Part IV, attempts to cast some light on the subject of personality and protection. While we are strong proponents of the "hard skills" of family security, e.g., learning best-in-class protective procedures and being able to physically intervene when required, we believe these are necessary but not sufficient to enable sustainable program success and keep clients productive and happy – in addition to safe. Therefore, we dedicate this last section to the "soft skills" which, in our experience, differentiate high-performing agents from the rest.

Finally, in the Appendix, we present a number of cases drawn from our years in protecting high net worth individuals and families. These brief stories illustrate the kinds of service professional security providers deliver on an ongoing basis.

We hope this book will help everyone involved in high net worth security – whether protector, protectee, or other stakeholders – to ask better, more critical questions about the best way to design, run, and improve protection programs. And we hope this book will, even in a small way, contribute to the further professionalization of our industry.

Bellevue, WA, USA
November 2018

Christian West
Brian Jantzen
Ivor Terret
Jared Van Driessche

5

Part I:
Foundations of family protective security

Introduction to Part I

The first section of this book explores the foundations of protective security for high net worth individuals and families.

Part I begins with the story of Bob, an entrepreneur turned sudden billionaire when his company's valuation jumped through the roof. Although Bob's story has been completely anonymized, we base it on the experiences of many of our clients. Like Bob, increased wealth and prominence changed their need for personal security, eventually leading to the kinds of protection programs we present in this book.

It wasn't that Bob or any of our clients always dreamt about a life that included 24/7 personal protection. Quite the opposite. Bob only accepted increased security measures gradually, as the need for them became too great to ignore. He would have happily gone on without residential security details, security drivers, and close personal protection were it not for the growing prominence and wealth that were the results of his business' success.

For Bob and many other prominent high net worth people, the use of professional security services is a necessity, not a wish. Their inability to walk down a city street without being confronted by total strangers who want something from them is a fact of life, but not one of the nicer ones. And while we all worry about our loved ones' wellbeing, Bob's concerns for his wife and children were amplified by the elevated risks they faced.

From the story of Bob, we move on to Chapter 1, where we investigate why high net worth families such as Bob's consider enhanced security programs. Risk mitigation is the primary driver, of course, but the wish to pursue the kind of lifestyle they prefer as a family is also important, as is maintaining their privacy.

In Chapter 2, we introduce the four pillars of protection for high net worth individuals and families: physical security, technology, people, and procedures. As we will see, all four elements are necessary components of protective security. It is by understanding how the four pillars work with and impact each other that security managers can achieve the kind of protective security that best fits the family's lifestyle preferences.

The security of one's family is, of course, something that is very dear to all of us. So dear, in fact, that the issue can quickly become emotionally charged. Chapter 3 attempts to untangle feelings from facts when it comes to security. We do this by examining the cognitive biases that can cloud our perceptions and get in the way of good security decisions and presenting ways that are more likely to result in an objective evaluation of actual security needs and how best to meet them.

In Chapter 4, we look at the ecosystem of high net worth family security. Protective programs and staffs must cooperate with many different stakeholders in family offices and estate management – not only with the principal – in order to be successful. Just as security providers need to understand the roles of the many different stakeholders that surround the principals, these stakeholders need to understand what enhanced security programs are all about. Efficient communication is key and one of the most important things that distinguishes good protection programs from failures.

Chapter 5 examines the role of secure travel support in protection programs. Here, we argue that customized secure ground travel is the missing link between business or first-class air travel, high-end hotels, and all the other places that high net worth families and individuals might want to visit. Here, a little bit of risk mitigation goes a long way to keep people safe and productive while on the road.

In Chapter 6, we raise some of the thorny issues related to licensing, legal compliance, and personal protection – all things that vary widely from one place to another. To manage liability, those responsible for personal security need to know precisely what is required and allowed in all relevant jurisdictions, and how regulations impact specific security services in specific contexts. What is legal in one place might not be in another. What is good, acceptable practice in one situation might expose you to legal risks and civil suits in another. They all matter, and many family protection programs have unwittingly run afoul of the law, exposing themselves to expensive and unnecessary lawsuits.

We close Part I with a chapter on the role of intelligence analysis in high net worth protection programs. Once reserved only for governmental or military protection programs, many corporations now employ intelligence analysts, too. In Chapter 7, we explain why we believe the time has come to broaden the purview of intelligence analysts to include the protection of high net worth individuals and families. We are already using this in many of our programs, and we are convinced that as the complexity of risk mitigation increases, intelligence analysis will prove its worth in even more of them.

The story of Bob

Bob never really wanted to be extremely wealthy. Things just worked out that way, as they sometimes do with talented entrepreneurs. He was highly intelligent, creative and crazy about coding. He had a good idea; the timing was right. If you asked Bob, he'd just say he got lucky. The real geniuses aren't usually the ones who claim to be smart.

As the founder of what would become a highly successful startup and then a major corporation, Bob worked hard and a lot. Still, he found time to pursue other interests like riding his mountain bike, cooking and hanging out with friends. Despite the ever-growing valuations of his company, he considered himself to be a "regular Joe" and disdained what he considered to be the affectations of the super rich: drivers, personal chefs, security and all the rest.

The money piled in and Bob felt good sharing it. He donated to charities and would even walk down the street handing out $100 bills to homeless people. There were thousands of them in his city and while he knew he couldn't help all of them, passing out some C-notes every once in a while seemed the least he could do.

Soon enough, word of the guy with lots of money spread on the street. Crowds of people would gather when Bob was around. He began to be recognized almost everywhere he went, and people seemed to like to interact with him – for their own reasons, of course, not Bob's. After someone got hold of his cell phone number, Bob started to get a few odd calls from strangers, then many. Most of the calls had to do with requests for money and favors; others offered unwanted business advice; some were antagonistic. None made him feel any better.

Bob didn't enjoy the incessant attention. In fact, it made him uneasy and eventually anxious. He changed his phone number and stopped handing out cash on the street. But the level of public scrutiny only grew as his company went from success to success, his personal wealth skyrocketed, and the media shined an ever-larger spotlight on him.

Overtures from obscure "friends" and acquaintances became commonplace. His company's HR department began to require background checks and screenings for new employees. Unsolicited investment opportunities poured in. Lawyers started talking about liabilities that Bob had never even considered imaginable; now he had to protect himself from them. How was he suddenly responsible for so many potential mishaps?

Bob had been exposed to security at corporate events but wanted nothing to do with it in his private life. He didn't think he was special enough for any bad guys to be particularly interested in him, and who wanted all those goonish looking bodyguards around? He enjoyed his lifestyle and didn't want to be encumbered by worries about his safety or any extra security measures.

Still, when he built a new home, he agreed to his company's and contractor's advice that the building site get some guards: Leaving the building site and increasingly valuable fixtures unwatched at night was a risk the contractor didn't want to take, and he couldn't have his own tradespeople stay there 24/7.

What began as security for a construction site became full-time residential security. Bob's wife didn't want to deal with all the strangers knocking on the door of their new home; she felt insecure when he was away. By the time his house was completed, Bob was not just rich but super rich and very well known. His company was often in the press, and although he didn't look for controversy, his views became news. He couldn't go anywhere without being recognized. Even when he was riding a bike, people had no hesitation in chatting him up and slowing him down. He could be accosted on the street and challenged publicly for almost anything – even in front of his young children.

That was the turning point in terms of his perception of personal security: He had become so prominent that he could no longer get away with being the regular Joe that he still felt like and wanted to be. He and his family were fair game to strangers, passersby and cranks. He hadn't wanted any security because he felt it would put a cramp on his lifestyle, but all the unwanted attention and attendant hassles were having an even bigger impact on how he wanted to live.

It was Bob's company that first required that he have close protection – initially at public events and when he traveled to high-risk countries, then more and more. As time went on and both his company's and his own prominence grew, Bob's executive protection coverage became the rule rather than the exception. It expanded to wherever he traveled, including the commute to and from work, and to his family as well.

Chapter 1:
Why high net worth families consider enhanced personal security

The story above has been changed "to protect the innocent" as they say, but its trajectory is true to the facts that face many of our clients. While all were aiming for the success of their business ventures and certainly wanted to make money, moving from unknown to celebrity status was more of an unintended consequence than a goal in itself.

Prominence came with the territory of business success and proved to be a double-edged sword. The notoriety and media coverage boost the value of corporate brands, but it also comes with personal costs for founders and CEOs: privacy in the first instance, but eventually and even more importantly, their own personal security and that of their families. The need for more security, and eventually, close personal protection evolved as prominence grew.

Unlike other perks of wealth, nobody aspires to have personal protection

No matter how you stack Maslow's hierarchy of needs[1], security is a fundamental requirement for people and families everywhere. Once we get beyond food, water and shelter, security is what matters most.

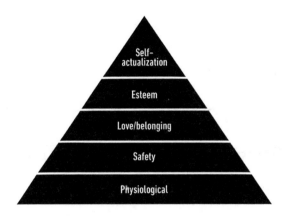

Maslow refers to safety and security in several ways, including avoiding accidents and illnesses, and achieving financial, health, and personal security. When we are "safe enough", we move on to meet higher needs. When we are not safe enough, we experience stress or even trauma – serious impediments to other endeavors such as self-actualization and all the other nice stuff. And as we will see in Chapter 3, feeling safe and being safe are not the same.

For high net worth families, however, the concept of security presents some special considerations. Their affluence

---

[1] Maslow, A.H. (1943). "A Theory of Human Motivation". In Psychological Review, 50 (4), 430-437. Washington; illustration by Daniel Leclercq.

obviously ensures that they have relative financial security and will receive the best medical care obtainable. Their circumstances preclude many of the misfortunes that might befall those who are less well off.

Having a lot of money enables better personal security in obvious ways, such as the neighborhoods where one lives and the types of risks one faces there. But relative wealth – and especially the prominence that often accompanies it – also turns individuals and families into particularly attractive targets for all kinds of crimes for financial gain, including home invasions and kidnappings.

Three reasons high net worth families opt for enhanced protective security: Risk mitigation, lifestyle and privacy

Every family seeks to lead the kind of life that makes them the happiest and most productive versions of themselves while minimizing the risks that could threaten their wellbeing. High net worth families do so, too, of course, and their needs for security mirror those of all families in two important ways: risk mitigation and lifestyle preferences. Due their prominence, however, they add a third: privacy.

1. Risk mitigation

Most folks get by with decent locks on their doors and some degree of street smarts. This mitigates known risks just fine – until it doesn't. The next steps might be an off-the-shelf alarm system or a dog, which could also work fine – until they don't.

Depending on available resources, this escalation can continue *ad infinitum*. But not even the most draconian security setup could ever eliminate all risks. The only way to do that would be to lock the family inside a fortress, never let them out or anyone else in, and have the U.S. Air Force establish a no-fly zone around the residence. Hardly the kind of lifestyle most people want.

Effective protective security is all about mitigating identified risks to manageable levels with available resources. This enables the security apparatus to reduce the opportunity to commit a hostile act on the protectees as early as possible in the attack cycle – sometimes still in the planning stages – and minimize damage from probable and critical risks that cannot be prevented.

While protective security cannot remove the chance of every imaginable harm, it does seek to identify and then minimize the likelihood of the most probable and critical risks.

Risk mitigation seeks to establish an acceptable balance between:

- Minimizing the probability and impact of identified risks to a level that makes us safe

- The resources (costs, time) required to do so, and

- The impact of security procedures on one's lifestyle

The starting point for any serious risk mitigation effort is the Risk, Threat, and Vulnerability Analysis (RTVA). Unless you comprehend the threats facing you and your vulnerabilities to these threats, you have no way of measuring risk – or understanding how to mitigate it.

Security experts love to split hairs when defining "threat", "vulnerability" and "risk". Here is our attempt at some simple definitions and how the concepts work together when it comes to protective programs.

Threats that are outside of our control are potentials for harm. Persons, groups, communicable diseases, socioeconomic trends, or even ideas might all represent threats to someone depending on contexts, circumstances and perspectives. A terrorist attack could cause great harm; so could a hurricane. We can't control either, but we can try to understand their probability and the criticality of their impact.

Vulnerability refers to our exposure to specific, probable and critical threats. How open are we to these sources of potential harm? How easily would a determined adversary or just bad luck compromise our defenses? Although we can do something about vulnerabilities, pretending to exercise complete control over every vulnerability is a fool's errand.

Risk is what you get when you when you map probable, critical threats to vulnerabilities that may provide opportunity for these threats to actualize. Risk determination begins with clear-eyed understanding of relevant threats then proceeds to an honest assessment of our vulnerabilities to these threats. If the probability and likely impact of a threat are high, and our vulnerability to such threats is also significant, then we are facing a quantifiable, elevated risk that requires mitigation.

Comprehensive RTVAs are the foundation of effective and cost-effective security

The RTVA process results in a security master plan. It incorporates all available factors to produce a client-specific, risk-based security model. An often time-consuming and complex undertaking, the resulting security master plan will include physical and technological risk mitigation measures along with manpower specifications and procedures to prevent and limit damage from hostile acts.

These RTVAs are based on probable and critical threats and are designed to negate correlating vulnerabilities. As eliminating all threats all the time is not possible, the RTVA process allows the security apparatus to focus resources on addressing vulnerabilities to the most probable and critical threats, thus mitigating risk as efficiently as possible in the given circumstances.

In most cases, we believe that at least some RTVA is better than no RTVA. The temptation to jump to conclusions without having gone through the effort of analyzing available facts is just as strong in the security field as it is in any other. Cookie-cutter solutions that give the illusion of security without actually mitigating risk abound, and plenty of companies sell them every day.

Solid RTVAs that are kept fresh through timely updates enable better decisions. Here are the basic questions they answer concerning security for high net worth families:

- Are there direct threats to the family or individuals? Has anyone provided overt or covert signs of intent to harm, extort, embarrass, etc.?

- Are there indirect threats not expressly targeting the family but present in places or contexts in which the family lives, works, travels?

- What would be the impact, or loss, should these threats be realized?

- What are the factors that cause or multiply threats? Prominence, opportunity, motivation?

- How vulnerable are we to these threats should they be realized?

- How do we assess security vulnerabilities?

- What can be done to reduce vulnerability?

- What is the status/evaluation of our current security and protection programs?

- Evaluation of current and past security and protection efforts: What lessons have we learned?

- What parts of the family office ecosystem are relevant to the protective effort? Who are the key stakeholders in the program's success?

- What are the principal's personal preferences regarding protection, privacy, and his or her lifestyle?

- Gap analysis: Where we are now compared to our goals?

2. Lifestyle preferences

Security can enable one's lifestyle or hamper it. Too much of the wrong kind of security impinges upon one's quality of life. So, does too little of the right kind. Like all other value propositions, the perceived value of enhanced security depends on the relationship between its costs and benefits. Are the results worth the tradeoffs? Again, it's a question of balance.

If we perceive the emotional costs of more security (loss of personal freedom, standing out socially) to be greater than the emotional benefits it brings (risk mitigation and peace of mind), then things are out of balance. As we saw in the case above, "Bob" wanted nothing to do with security because he didn't want it to impose on his preferred lifestyle. He was a regular Joe (OK, a rather wealthy regular Joe) who enjoyed the kind of life he'd led since his early twenties and had no desire to encumber it with more security. He could see the emotional costs of security but perceived no need for its benefits.

As all the hassles and worries due to his growing prominence escalated, however, Bob changed his mind. The tipping point came when he realized that he and his family could no longer maintain their preferred lifestyle without security. The balance had changed. The family's prominence resulted in an increasingly uncomfortable lack of privacy and sense of insecurity; the prominence was not going to go away anytime soon; ergo, something else had to change. Bob and his family restored balance by adding security. The tradeoffs turned out to be manageable and, with the right people, completely acceptable.

3. Privacy

Prominent individuals and families have a third motivation for security that sometimes trumps the others: privacy.

Whether they've made their fortune in high-profile fields such as entertainment or sports, are powerful players in closely scrutinized industries, or scions of established families, they are well known if not outright "celebrities". While this might seem an attractive perk to some, the more prominent a person or family, the more likely they are to be approached by strangers.

In almost all cases, such interactions are unwanted. They can range from slight to enormous invasions of privacy (chatting up the principal, photography of the principal and family at private events, getting "pied" at public events). They include troublesome but largely innocuous exchanges with strangers (you're rich, I'm not – how about giving me some of your money?). They can also be hostile threats or outright crimes (assault, stalking, kidnapping of the principal or his/her family).

Who decides on what good security is? The family, of course.

We admit it: No one truly wants protective services. At least not in the way people want other consequences of wealth like financial freedom, nice homes and wonderful vacations. But given the way our world works, some high net worth individuals and families truly need enhanced security.

As we saw in Bob's case, it is ultimately the family that determines what "mitigating risk to an acceptable level" means and entails. They can do this from an informed point of view based on a solid RTVA or on impulse. They can get outside help. Or they can do it on gut feelings.

As private sector security professionals, we can have opinions and even expert opinions. We can argue for our viewpoints. But we don't get to decide. The family decides. This is one of the things that distinguishes private sector protection from public sector protection, where security protocols are followed much more strictly, with or without the principal's acquiescence.

What actually causes a high net worth person or family to initiate or increase close protection can be many things. It can be an unpleasant incident or repeated threats by a person of interest. A fresh RTVA might give reasons to re-evaluate the current setup. Corporate security might recommend it. A board of directors might mandate it.

In practically all cases, a tipping point has been reached and there is an imbalance that needs to be corrected. Status quo security arrangements are no longer considered sufficient to mitigate perceived risks, protect privacy, or enable the family's preferred lifestyle.

When striking the optimal balance between a security program's costs and benefits, it is important to remember that the emotional dimensions can be just as important – if not more so than financial considerations. Feelings are also real.

As we learned from Maslow, the emotional benefits of having "good enough" security are profound and essential for us to pursue the kinds of lives we find most fulfilling. There are emotional costs involved with having too little security as well as having too much of the wrong kinds of security. So much the better when the determination of what is "good enough" is based on facts and expert opinion, not feelings. While no CEO would do without legal counsel, this is often not the case when it comes to their own personal security.

In financial terms, it's no surprise that the highest quality security costs more than the lowest quality. Tailor-made alarm systems designed by the best and brightest will be more expensive than cookie-cutter solutions you can find at the local hardware store and install yourself. Expert protection by highly trained agents is costlier than a couple of guys from the local guard company making minimum wage.

But just as there is a market for both high-end luxury cars and low-end compacts, as long as there is a balance between perceived costs and perceived benefits, both will sell.

High net worth families like Bob's don't necessarily possess better emotional resources than anyone else, but they do have the financial resources to seek out and acquire the kinds of security that minimize lifestyle hassles and invasions of privacy while maximizing risk mitigation.

Our next chapters will take a closer look at how this can be done skillfully.

Chapter 2:
The four pillars of protection for high net worth individuals and families

In this chapter, we introduce the four foundational elements of protection for high net worth individuals and families: physical security, technology, people, and procedures.

Our goal is to provide an overview of these four main elements, not an exhaustive description of each. Rather, we hope to point to how the various components of protective security are interrelated, and that by better understanding how these components work with and impact each other, families will be better able to achieve the kind of protective security that best fits their lifestyle preferences.

The four protective pillars provide a stable protective platform – as long as they are integrated effectively

Effective security depends on striking the optimal balance between people, procedures, technology, and physical security. Compartmentalization and over reliance on one element – to the detriment of another – creates imbalance and the potential for protective failure.

In our experience, technology is what people rely on most, with little consideration for the other three legs of a balanced platform. Standard alarm systems, for example, can be a general deterrent against less experienced burglars. But they do little to hinder a determined hostile. Similarly, a sophisticated alarm system that is not supported by well-trained personnel employing proven operating procedures is also of questionable value. Even if the alarm does go off, if emergency response takes 10 minutes or more, an intruder could gain entrance, commit his crime, and be off again. Likewise, high-definition cameras might capture excellent images of masked intruders, but such videos do not mitigate the risk of intrusion if no one is watching the monitor and prepared to react and intervene.

Careful coordination of all four elements, on the other hand, enables security that is both effective and in alignment with how family members want to live their lives.

1. Technology and physical security

Technology alerts us to a security issue or helps with follow-up investigations. Physical security creates time and distance between a hostile and the family and limits the damage caused should an interaction occur. The two have separate purposes and are used differently. They also require different skill sets, people and procedures.

Homes are different than corporate campuses. We want them to be secure without feeling like fortresses or, even worse, prisons. Most families thus refuse technological and physical security commonly used in office and factory buildings. Barbed wire fences, turnstiles, metal detectors and biometric devices might be fine if that's what security requires at work – but not at home. Such trappings of corporate security are nothing most families want to expose their children, friends, or neighbors to.

Below, we'll take a quick look at the three layers of physical security and some of the most commonly used technology to protect each level. Our goal here is not to recommend who should have what kind of physical security. This can only be done case-by-case and based on a good risk, threat, vulnerability analysis. Rather, we hope to provide an overview of the most common technological building blocks and how they are integrated in layers of physical security.

The perimeter around the property

- Property perimeters can be protected by fences and walls, as well as natural landscape features

- Access control to the property such as gates, driveways and bollards

- Lights that illuminate critical areas

- Intrusion detection sensors, including photoelectric, ultrasonic, infrared, etc., that alert the presence of people around the property's pcrimeter

- Closed circuit TVs (CCTVs) with smart analytic software that provides live and taped feeds of perimeter areas

The shell of the house

- Barriers to the outside such as walls, windows and doors – all of which can be standard design or "hardened" to provide enhanced protection from break-ins or ballistics

- Access control in the form of robust locks for windows and doors or bars on windows

- Lights

- Intrusion detection sensors, including photoelectric, ultrasonic, infrared, etc., that alert the presence of people around the house

- Closed circuit TV systems with smart analytic software that provides live and taped feeds of perimeter areas

The cell within the house – rooms and other interior spaces

- Barriers between areas of the house such as secure doors

- Safe rooms with reinforced doors and walls, communication equipment to call for help, first aid, etc.

- Intrusion detection sensors, including photoelectric, ultrasonic, infrared, etc., that alert the presence of people within the house

- Closed circuit TV systems that provide live and taped feeds of the house's interior areas

- Back-up power: Much of the technology used for protection depends on electricity to function. Back-up power is a must in case of power outages due to natural causes or perpetration by hostiles.

2. The interplay between technology, the three layers of physical security, and personal preferences

When families and their specialist security partners appreciate the relationships and interdependencies between architecture, technology and physical security, they are more likely to design solutions that maximize security and minimize hassles. Aesthetic and lifestyle preferences should play a key role here, too.

This starts with understanding the interdependencies and overlaps between technology and the three levels of physical security outlined above: perimeter, shell and cell. All three are critical to security, of course, and any of the three can be designed to be more or less "hard" depending on the strength of the other two. The overlaps between the three layers can strengthen overall security; conversely, gaps between the layers – at points where they meet and interact – can prove to be a security system's weakest points.

A residence that is secure by design, such as Bob's newly built house, is precisely that. Security by design often reduces the need for security staff, saves a lot of money in the medium and long terms – and is usually much more aesthetically pleasing.

If a home's boundaries are completely impregnable, for example, then its shell needn't be. An unassailable property perimeter might work fine if you're defending a military base but would not be appropriate in most suburban neighborhoods. Even the White House, arguably one of the best-protected residences on the planet, guards its perimeter with a fence that has been scaled many times by intruders. The U.S. government obviously has the means to erect a barrier that would stop anyone in his tracks. However, aesthetic, historical, and cultural values dictate a less imposing impediment, so the Secret Service depends on additional protective means in the form of technology, other physical security measures, trained people, and proven procedures.

When designers and specialist security partners work closely together early in the design process, they create solutions better suited to the family's aesthetic and lifestyle preferences. For example, walls and lighting can appear as attractive architectural expressions rather than unsightly afterthoughts. Families that like to greet guests at the door rather than through a CCTV system can install glass doors (highly secure and bullet-proof – without looking it) so they can see who's knocking without exposing themselves to risk.

3. The human element of protective security: People

The most important factor in effective security is people, period. Security would be simple if you could just buy some tech gear, program it according to a smart algorithm and let it run. But security depends on people, with all our brilliant advantages and frustrating drawbacks included.

When protective security succeeds in foiling an attack by a determined hostile, it's because people did the right things in the right way at the right time. Conversely, responsibility for failures is ultimately always assigned to one or more persons – not to a failed piece of tech or a faulty procedural playbook. It's always up to people to spec and test the tech; whether teams develop and follow effective preventative and emergency procedures also depends on people.

Family offices should consider the importance of people in a least three ways when it comes to protective security.

a. Make sure the people responsible for organizing protective security have relevant, proven experience, and expertise

Evaluating the expertise of specialists in a domain that is not your own can be difficult, if not impossible. Protective security is definitely such a domain for most high net worth individuals and families. So how can family offices find the people they will entrust with planning and implementing personal security?

In our experience, there are two main methods, each at its own end of the spectrum, and lots of variations in between. We'll let you decide which one works best for you.

The "I got a guy" method: Let's be honest – this is how a lot of things get done everywhere. You have a leaky sink and you go through your internal Rolodex until you recall your neighbor's cousin is a plumber and he's the first one you call. Or maybe your Rolodex comes up blank, so you call your neighbor and ask for a tip. Why?

First, because it's quick and easy. Second, because you may have met him before and he seemed like a decent guy. Third, he might cut you a deal, or will at least be unlikely to cheat you because he's connected to your network.

That's all great, but there's not much due diligence or best-practice procurement procedure about it. Maybe there doesn't need to be, either, for a leaky sink. But for personal security?

When it comes to security, the "guy" might be an ex-law enforcement officer, military veteran, government employee, or executive protection agent. They might have all kinds of security experience, but no specific expertise working with families in residential or close protection.

Specialist partners: At the other end of the spectrum is another approach. This, too, entails reaching out to others for counsel. But instead of taking the first and best opinions, it starts with some benchmarking questions.

Who are the specialist partners that provide security services to comparable families or family offices? How do they organize security? Whom do the people you trust recommend?

Once you've boiled down the universe of possible partners to a handful, then it's time to request some proposals. We'll dig into this process in Chapter 16 and provide some tips on how to distinguish between those who take a risk-based approach to protective security and those who apply cookie-cutter methods.

b. Demand transparent and reliable recruitment procedures for all security staff

In a system that is only as strong as its weakest link, it's vitally important to hire trustworthy people with the right credentials. Here, two issues arise, competencies and trust.

Competencies, training, and qualifications: The folks you found in the previous step – the experienced experts who will help you organize your protective security program – will be the ones to help you determine program staffing requirements.

Actual qualifications and competencies will depend on what kind of program and staff you require. We will dig into the details of this in a later chapter, but families who need protection should demand full transparency into how staff vetting takes place and understand the importance of relevant training.

It is tempting to be impressed by security agents who boast advanced proficiency in everything from martial arts to underwater knife fighting. But training for security team members must focus on preventative and emergency procedures for risks that are probable and critical.

If we have procedures for responding to a fire, for example, do agents have the training to use the extinguishers on property? Do they know when to use them and when to leave things to the local fire department? What about other standard operating procedures for residential security? Does everyone know what to do and how to do it?

Trust: You need trustworthy men and women on the security team, but how do you know whom to trust? To quote Vladimir Lenin, "Trust is good, control is better".

At the outset, thorough vetting and background checks are the minimum. Psychological tests, aptitude tests, and polygraphs can also be used – depending on need and jurisdiction.

As programs continue to evolve, ongoing background checks are often a good idea. You want to know if a current staff member has stepped out of agreed bounds while not on the job – for example, if a security driver has any new traffic violations.

c. Require ongoing quality assurance and improvement programs for key people

It's the responsibility of security teams to make sure nothing happens to the principal. Fortunately, nothing usually happens.

Does this mean the security team is doing a good job following predefined procedures or just lucky? Are procedures and skills up-to-date and stress-tested? Are team members calmly competent or inexcusably complacent? How can you ever know?

Quality assurance programs are the only way managers have a chance to evaluate team preparedness. Such programs include standard operating procedure (SOP) reviews, announced and unannounced audits, red teaming and stakeholder feedback.

Ongoing training is also an important component of team readiness. Some critical skills, e.g. CPR and first aid, are perishable and need to be refreshed on a regular basis if they are to be relied upon.

4. Reliable procedures bind people and physical deterrents together

The fourth protective pillar concerns procedures: The protocols, processes and established ways of doing things that bind together skilled people and effective physical deterrents to provide consistently effective security.

Procedures are divided into two categories:

a. Routine procedures

These are the day-to-day preventative activities the team conducts to identify a potential offender as early and as far from the family as possible. These procedures should be designed to negate critical and probable threats and should not hinder the family's daily activities or the home's normal comings and goings.

It is critical that routine procedures and emergency procedures support and build on each other. For example, if emergency procedure dictates that a gate be locked, then routine procedure must ensure that there is a gate; that the gate and the lock are in good working order; that the role of gate-locker-in-emergency is assigned, understood, trained, and controlled; that the key is in the designated location, etc. It sounds obvious. You'd be surprised.

b. Emergency or crisis procedures

These are designed to stop an imminent or occurring hostile act at the earliest possible stage and as far away as possible from the family. When called for, these procedures take priority over routine procedures, containing threats and limiting damage as quickly and decisively as possible.

Security managers and team leads should write and maintain sets of standard operating procedures and key performance indicators (KPIs) for routine and emergency processes. While we expect that all business people will be familiar with the concepts, we will highlight below some of the reasons why clear, actionable SOPs and KPIs are so critical to security work.

Focus and accountability: It's no surprise that people perform best when they know what is expected of them. What is startling is that so many employees are in doubt, as surveys often reveal that many employees are in doubt about exactly what is expected of them at work.

There is no room for such doubts on security teams. Everyone must know exactly what he or she should be doing – along with when things are to be done, how they should be done and where they need to happen. You want security people who can think, of course, but you don't want them getting creative with SOPs unless these are under review – never on a daily basis.

Reduced learning curve: Good SOPs make it easier for security team members to learn their jobs. We don't ask residential agents to learn every aspect of residential security on day one. We train them to be 100% effective at the specific tasks they are assigned – and follow the associated SOPs closely. It's thus possible to get agents up-to-speed quickly so that they can perform their part of the overall security reliably and consistently – and then learn how to perform other parts.

Substitutability and continuity: Good SOPs ensure continuity since everyone can rely on everyone else to do as prescribed and expected. This is absolutely critical in security work, where a weak link in the protective chain can lead not just to lower productivity, but to mission failure. Good SOPs also enhance substitutability so that team members can take on a variety of different roles.

Quality control, audits and performance reviews: Finally, it's important to remember that SOPs and KPIs can be used to prescribe as well as evaluate performance. Prescriptively, SOPs stipulate what is to be done. For evaluation purposes, KPIs based on SOPs are used to assess the health of the protective program overall, understand how individual team members are performing, check whether our own processes are effective, and where not, fix them.

Quality control and auditing aim to identify where people and procedures require improvement. It's not so much a question of "finding the bad apple" as it is a preventative measure to expose gaps in our own processes, including recruitment, training, procedures, suitability of equipment, use of equipment, integrity, etc. Quality control and auditing must be followed up with corrective action to ensure that lessons learned are implemented, thus ensuring a constantly improving state of readiness.

Chapter 3:
Separating feelings from facts: What high net worth families need to understand to stay secure

Both feelings and facts influence our sense of security, but sometimes we have a hard time distinguishing between the two.[2] Why? Because we feel first and think later – sometimes way later. And if we do ever get around to thinking about security,

---

[2] For more information on this subject, please see Terret, Ivor, MSc, security protection specialist, researcher, and counter-terror educator. Research publication:
https://drive.google.com/file/d/1QQtrBInhTHLMfYMgeRFDvkOW-wmR5x27u/view

then inexperience and a host of preconceived notions can all combine to cloud our view and lead to poor decisions.

In this chapter, we take a look at what high net worth families – and any other family, really – can do about it to make better fact-based decisions about their security needs.

The process starts with acknowledging a lack of security expertise and understanding some of our cognitive biases. We then need to become more aware of the trade-offs between enhancing security and limiting lifestyle choices – and review our options using transparent criteria.

The differences between perceived and actual security are not obvious, and you can't always tell which conditions cause which outcomes. But even if you have no objective means of determining whether or why you're safe, you can still have plenty of feelings one way or another. And yes, also security "experts" are influenced by feelings and perceptions.

You can be relatively secure even if you don't feel that way. Just think of how many people are afraid of flying but have absolutely no worries when it comes to driving, then compare the statistics for both. Commercial air travel is clearly the safest way to get from A to B and you're far more likely to die in a car crash, but a lot of people still feel way more insecure when flying than driving.

The converse is also true, of course: We might be less secure, objectively speaking, than our feelings would lead us to believe. To stick with the driving example, it is striking to note that 83% of drivers consider themselves to be more careful than the average driver, 16% see themselves as average, and less than 1% rate themselves as below average. Really? Really.

We've run into plenty of hard-nosed business people who demand nothing but fact-based decision making at work, then consistently rely on feelings when it comes to their personal security. Like Bob, they might feel like an ordinary Joe despite sudden and massive prominence and therefore reject (or at least stay stubbornly unaware of) the fact that highly prominent people are more exposed to security risks than others.

Still, feelings do matter when it comes to security. If one or more persons in a family feel insecure and unprotected in the face of perceived threats (just as Bob's wife felt insecure when her husband was out of town), then this causes anxiety and reduces their quality of life. Indeed, the presence of a lot of security staff – especially the less professional teams that make an overt show of themselves – can also bring on feelings of insecurity. On the other hand, unrealistic feelings of invulnerability might prevent people from acknowledging actual threats and taking appropriate countermeasures to mitigate them. This exposes them and others to unnecessary risks.

Some security activities straddle the gap between perception and reality with "security theater": They provide the illusion of effective security but not the authenticity of effective risk mitigation or forceful response in case of emergency. This isn't always a bad thing. After 9/11, armed members of the National Guard appeared in many U.S. airports bearing weapons that were sometimes unloaded. But their purpose was as much to reassure a jittery public as it was to deter attacks and provide first response. Such deployments can make good sense.

But security theater isn't always smart. Cookie cutter alarm systems are a case in point: They often don't work as promised; they are easy for real pros to circumvent; they are so inconvenient that people end up turning them off. They don't actually prevent home invasions, but they can create an illusion of safety that is far worse than the real thing if push comes to shove. The same goes for some residential and other security guards we have audited: Teams can be complacent, unmotivated and fail to follow even the most ineffective standard operating procedures, even though they are on site. As principals have no obvious means of discovering this, they might feel safe even though their security program in place is not contributing much more than theatrics.

After a combined 80+ years in the protective security industry, our bottom line is this: If you feel safe, you probably won't want to do anything about your security situation. If you feel unsafe, you probably will. Unfortunately, some security providers are not above using scare tactics to influence perceptions. Ultimately, however, the family's feelings on the issues are the only evaluation that matters. If they want additional security, they'll get it. If they don't want it, they won't get it.

Nonetheless, we believe families can and should learn to make better security choices informed by both feelings and facts. To do that, they need to understand their own limitations and get some outside help.

Five cognitive biases cloud our perception of security needs – and get in the way of good decisions

Whether on the road or at home, most people are under-informed about the security risks that actually face them. The probability of threats and their potential damage – the classical anchor points of risk analysis – are poorly understood. Instead, we rely on snap judgments brought to us by our emotions and shaped by our cognitive biases. Let's look at some of the psychological predispositions that affect our security decisions.

1. The optimism bias: We humans seem to be hardwired for optimism when predicting what's going to happen in the future. We overestimate the probability of good outcomes and underestimate the likelihood of bad ones.

Don't get us wrong – we generally prefer to see the glass as half-full rather than half-empty. But when it comes to risk analysis, we prefer realism to either pessimism or optimism. Most high net worth individuals will admit that is (or ought to be) true for investment and business continuity risks. In our business, we know it is also true regarding personal security risks.

2. The spectacular bias: What's statistically riskier fades to insignificance next to something that's spectacular but unlikely to happen again soon. Air crashes make national news, fortunately very rarely, but when's the last time you read that 40,000 people died in traffic accidents last year in the U.S. alone?

Another example: We know of people who cancel trips to Europe due to rare but actual terror attacks in some countries there, but happily travel to developing countries, where the risk of injury in traffic is far greater than the U.S., and car accidents happen every single day, without ever considering hiring a vetted driver.

3. The zero-risk bias: Investment pros are familiar with this one. We tend to reduce some risks to zero even though it might be smarter to decrease other, more impactful risks to a lesser extent – and thus lower overall risk with the same costs. It's easy to understand with money: Leaving assets in a bank account means zero risk of losing them, but it also means zero or very low returns. This concept can be harder to grasp with security.

A zero-risk approach to personal security might lead people to completely eschew travel to some places despite their business or personal interest. A more balanced approach would enable such journeys through proven risk mitigation means and thus allow the achievement of business and personal goals despite the apparent risks.

4. The unknown bias: Psychologists have long known that we tend to trust the familiar and distrust the unfamiliar. This no doubt made sense when our ancestors were faced with unusual plants (to eat or not to eat?) or a new group of guys with wooden clubs in our territory (to fight or to flee?) But it doesn't always help in our modern, globalized world.

We feel that we are in control in the familiar situations where we spend most of our time. These might, in fact, be the riskiest because they provide the highest levels of predictable opportunity for those who wish us ill.

In the same way, principals might think twice about hotel security when traveling to far-off places, yet be perfectly happy with an off-the-shelf (and largely ineffective) home alarm system, even though they may live in an area with high crime rates. Their companies would never hire consultants without having first checked out their reputations, but we often can and do hire nannies and other household help without thorough background checks.

5. The control bias: We typically downplay risks when we believe we are in control of the situation and overrate them in situations that we don't feel we control. Unless you're a pilot, driving versus flying comes to mind again, but there are other instances we often run into in our line of business.

For example, we know of principals who hire extra residential security guards if they are away while the wife and kids remain at home, then let them go as soon as Dad is back. This is great, but what would Dad actually do to thwart a determined home invasion in progress? We also know high net worth individuals who would never dream of driving a rental car in Nigeria or India, but don't think twice about driving themselves to and from work – and staying on top of emails while at the wheel.

The combination of naiveté and cognitive biases makes an unfortunate security cocktail. You don't know what you don't know, and that might mean trouble.

Facts matter, too. Talking more about the RTVA

While emotions matter and should always be acknowledged, there are ways to bring rational thinking into the security equation. As we saw in Chapter 1, we believe the best way to do this is to perform a Risk, Threat, and Vulnerability Analysis (RTVA) that includes both qualitative and quantitative assessments.

Our RTVAs are to security as SWOT analyses are to business. But whereas few CEOs would approve a business plan without having professionals analyze the strengths, weaknesses, opportunities and threats facing the venture, plenty have no problem making security decisions without any kind of RTVA.

These RTVAs are based on facts that can be independently verified against objective and agreed criteria and move beyond the realm of feelings. Depending on available resources, they can be exhaustive or cursory, performed in-house or by third parties. But the goal of the RTVA is always the same: to measure risk as comprehensively, accurately and actionably as possible.

Principals don't need to know all the details of the RTVA or security master plans, which spell out precisely how protective details are to work and interact with other elements of the security system. But they should understand the basic logic of risk mitigation and be consulted on how the consequences of the security master plan affects them practically and personally.

Three things families can do to make better informed security decisions

So, what can a family do about all of this? The solution is straightforward: Acknowledge your lack of expertise and get some qualified help, be aware of the trade-offs – and demand transparency from your security providers.

1. Find a specialist partner to help you with your security planning

Experience and expertise do make a difference in overcoming naiveté and cognitive biases. That's why high net worth families hire the best financial advisors to help with investments and the best lawyers to help with estate planning. They should consider retaining specialist security advisors to help them with security, too.

These outside advisors don't necessarily have to be the same ones that eventually provide the security services. But advisors should have a verifiable track record in starting up, turning around, and sustaining high-performance security programs for other families.

2. Choose the trade-offs between security and lifestyle that best suit you

There are no guarantees of permanent, absolute and unchanging safety in the real world. Security is always relative to surrounding conditions and available resources. But relatively good security is far, far better than relatively bad security – and there are ways to distinguish good from bad security.

Tradeoffs between security and freedom are a fact of life. It's true for governments and it's true for families. The benefits of enhanced security must be compared to the costs – be they financial or psychological in terms of limitations on freedom of movement or lifestyle choices.

Perfect security would mean zero exposure to any risk, ever. This works if you're willing to hunker down in your own version of Fort Knox and never again venture into the world, but who wants to do that? Even the president of the United States is never completely safe out in the world, even though he is protected 24/7 by vast security resources costing upwards of $2 million per day.

Extremely prominent high net worth individuals know that they can't move around the world with the same freedom as the rest of us. There are simply too many people that recognize them and want a piece of them for them to go to the supermarket whenever they feel like shopping. But like everyone else, they too want to get out and pursue their business and personal interests – and they want their children to be able to enjoy childhood and make their own way in the world with as much freedom as is safely possible.

In our experience, the least intrusive and most personalized security measures are often the most expensive in the short term but prove to be the best investment in the long term. For example, families will actually use a custom-made alarm system designed by security experts in collaboration with architects in the design phase of a new home or remodeling of an existing home, but often grow tired of plain vanilla alarms, even from "leading providers", and simply stop using them. Why? If alarms are cumbersome and unreliable, the hassle is not worth the perceived benefit.

Cookie-cutter security, as we have stressed earlier, is never better than customized security. Families that work with security providers that are responsive to their lifestyle preferences and can adapt best practices to the family's particular needs, are more likely to forge sustainable relationships with their security providers and stay safer. They also save time, trouble, and money by choosing top-tier security partners rather than having to recruit, train, fire – repeat – new ones all the time.

3. Demand transparency into the issues that matter

Since few families are security experts, it can be difficult for them to ask the right questions of prospective or current security providers. That doesn't mean these questions shouldn't be asked.

How do security providers vet employees and subcontractors? How happy is the family with the services provided? How do managers combat complacency among security staff when nothing usually happens (and that's a good thing)? How do they perform quality assurance? What are the key performance indicators they measure their own performance on? And how will they share these with you?

The family needn't know all the details, but those responsible for family security must. To do so, families must demand transparency, so they can look behind the curtains of their security providers and continue to be sure that they are getting the best risk mitigation possible for the available resources.

Chapter 4:
The ecosystem of high net worth family security: Four keys to understanding successful programs

As Leo Tolstoy pointed out, happy families are all alike, but unhappy families are all unhappy in their own ways. We believe the Anna Karenina[3] principle applies to the protection of high net worth families, too. But only if we turn it on its head.

To paraphrase Tolstoy: "Successful high net worth family protection programs are all different; unsuccessful programs usually fail for the same reasons". In this chapter, we'll examine

---

[3] Tolstoy, Leo, graf, 1828-1910. (1980). *Anna Karenina*. Oxford; New York: Oxford University Press.

the ecosystem of high net worth protection programs to understand the reasons why they succeed – and hopefully prevent program failure for more families.

The four keys to success

To achieve success in high net worth family protection, it is important to understand the ecosystems in which security services are provided for these families and individuals. These ecosystems comprise many different dynamics and stakeholders, the security team being only one part of a larger whole. All families are different, of course, and so are the ways the many interacting parts of a complex network operate together.

1. Customizing security to family culture and preferences starts with lots of questions and careful listening

Even executives who are used to some kind of protective services on the job can find security for the home and family bothersome at best and downright intrusive at worst. Putting up with outsiders at work is one thing. Having them close to family and friends at all times of the day is something else.

In our experience, the first step to a successful program is understanding the necessity of adapting security to the family's culture and individual preferences rather than the other way around. High net worth families are used to lots of customization options when it comes to many other aspects of their lives, and security should be no different. Neglecting to customize security practices to the family's individual needs and wants is a key cause of program failure.

While we're all for watertight standard operating procedures (SOPs) based on best practices, the reality is that these cannot simply be copy-pasted from one program to another. They need to be adapted to every new situation, especially when concerning the private sphere. And the best way to understand a family's culture and preferences is to stop talking and start listening.

Here are just a few of the questions that are important to ask:

Strangers at the gate – or inside the walls: How does the family feel about having a residential security team on the property? And does the risk warrant it?

Bringing strangers into the inner sanctum of the home, even if they are there to protect and are very professional, tests the personal boundaries of any family. This can be especially difficult for people new to security. The best way to deal with this issue is openly. Put the issues on the table, make transparent the pros and cons of different alternatives, and ask questions.

Is the family open to on-property security? To what extent and how? Can the residential security team roam the property to check up on things when time allows? When in the day? Do we need to stick to predefined routes or can we do random patrols? Are there areas that are off-limits to security, where the family insists on total privacy? If the family does not want security on the property, do we park on the street? Can we rent a house or apartment next door?

False alarm: What kinds of physical security equipment are used for security, and does the use of this equipment match the way the family lives?

Alarms, sensors and cameras are great security tools, but only if they get used. And they only get used if they are convenient and designed around the family's lifestyle and preferences. Cookie-cutter solutions that get tacked on to homes and family habits often end up being more bothersome than helpful, so they don't even get turned on.

How does the family use their current system? How does the equipment match their daily habits? How do family members typically greet guests – at the door or with a security camera? What would a parent actually do if he or she was awakened by an alarm in the middle of the night? Where would they go first?

Is the family OK with cameras? Where is it OK to record, and where is simple observation all that is allowable? What do we need to mask out as sensitive areas due to privacy?

What are the needs of all family members, spouses, young or teenage children? What about safety around pools and play areas?

For high net worth families that have security teams at their residences, it's important to remember that the tech is there to help the security team and should be run by them – not by the family. Basically, the tech should be seen as the team's extended eyes and ears, covering areas that team members do not, for one reason or another, cover with team members.

Larger, more complex protective teams will monitor all tech and provide other back-up services from an operations center. Whether this operations center is on the property or off depends, again, on the family's preferences as well as the property's physical layout.

Coordinating with other security elements: While residential security is typically a big part of high net worth security, it is not the only one. Security drivers and executive protection also play a role in many programs, and it's important that all pieces mesh together as seamlessly as possible as working parts of the security master plan.

How do family members feel about driving? What about spouses and teenage children? Do they want to drive themselves, or are security drivers needed for some or all trips? If principals do drive themselves, are discreet security escorts an option? What about GPS tracking?

Do any of the family members use executive protection sometimes or always? If there is an executive protection team, it is critical to understand its role, too, and to coordinate this with the other pieces of the security master plan. Administrative issues are one thing, as the executive protection team might be paid for and managed through the principal's corporation and separately from the residential team. Security issues are another thing: Whether the executive protection teams operate covertly or overtly, seamless protection is only possible when residential and executive protection teams cooperate closely – and understand exactly when and how handoffs take place.

2. High net worth security doesn't happen in a vacuum, so you have to know your stakeholders

Security teams need to determine the types and amounts of information that they can share with and receive from these teams. Establishing ground rules for sharing information so that the group avoids violating any family sensitivities is key. Again, the main idea is that we want everyone to be successful in providing their specific services to the family.

We have covered the corporate side of security extensively in our previous book, so we will not go into detail here. Still, it is important to note that high net worth security teams often need to interact with the principal's corporation, including executive administrative assistants (EAAs), corporate security departments and others, including intelligence analysts.

Family and residential security can be seen as a hindrance or an enabler depending on the relationships that are created. The goal is to always be seen as the enabler.

Proactive communication and planning are critical. Executive administrative assistants and members of various corporate departments might also liaise with residential security teams as needed. Executive administrative assistants do not want to feel that they must perform security duties in addition to their own. Regular meetings with EAAs to gather and share critical information will help the protection team provide recommendations and guide the protection support required. Such meetings are also an opportunity to address any concerns or questions the EAA staff might have about security.

The ecosystems of high net worth security comprise far more stakeholders than the family and protection professionals. To be successful, everyone on the security team must first understand all stakeholder roles and agendas, then respect and accommodate other stakeholders' needs as they go about their jobs.

Let's look at the main stakeholder categories and how they interact with protective security teams:

Family offices: Family offices help run the financial affairs of many high net worth families, typically handling the financial side of the family "business" from real estate acquisition to the management of the family's wealth. They also often help oversee the management of properties and may be directly or indirectly involved in hiring and liaising with security providers. There are two different configurations that you can encounter here – the single-family office and the multi-family office.

Security managers: Security managers must work closely with family offices on all financial and administrative issues, of course, but it is also important to keep them in the loop on all critical issues relating to program design and performance. Principals will often go through the family office when they want changes in their security, so it is key that family office managers, who are often our "clients", have excellent insight into what we are doing and why, and that any HR issues are shared with them in an open and timely way. Regular meetings to review administrative and other issues are highly recommended.

Estate management and staff: Estate management, which is responsible for the day-to-day operations of one or more residences, may or may not be part of the family office. In any case, estate management is a close working partner of estate security and must be treated as such. Estate management and staff are the stakeholders that residential security teams interact with most frequently, so smooth cooperation is absolutely essential.

This is an area in which the security team must do its job and help others be successful in doing theirs. The protection team should aspire to be seen as an enabler and partner of the entire estate staff. While establishing boundaries is also important, creating trust and partnership among the family staff is paramount. This can be managed with clear, consistent communication as well as operational and financial transparency, and an educational approach.

One area of collaboration is carrying out background checks for new staff hires. Another is developing and enforcing protocols for allowing craftspeople, caterers and other commercial guests access to the property. There are many more.

Security professionals need to understand that estate staff often have relationships with the principal family that go way back and can be intensely loyal. Cleaning personnel and gardeners may have been with the family for years or even generations. Young nannies might well be trusted more than a seasoned security manager with a black belt and military distinctions. Like all other stakeholders in the high net worth ecosystem, everyone on the estate staff – everyone – must be treated with the utmost respect, always. Read the Story of "Tom" in Part II.

Private aircraft and yacht/maritime staff: Traveling teams such as air and yacht crew often have intel about upcoming family plans before anyone else in the ecosystem.

Intelligence analysts may be tasked with understanding threats posed by persons or groups of interest or other factors. They might also be involved in monitoring online activities related to the principals, providing travel intelligence, and other analyses.

Finally, it is important to remember that everyone throughout the ecosystem can also be considered as part of the overall protective effort. Excellent collaboration between security professionals and others working in the household runs deep as well as wide.

Everyone can benefit from security awareness training, for example, whether it is housekeepers, gardeners, or the principal's spouse and children. Nannies with security driver training are much safer in traffic than those that have not received any special training. Fire safety and response training is relevant for all. And while tactical medical training should be required for security agents, other household staff members might be able to save lives if they, too, are properly trained.

Good security providers that want to become preferred partners add value not only on their own, but through working with everyone else in the ecosystem to raise the bar on comprehensive protective services.

3. Customize family security programs that are based on a good understanding of stakeholder needs, professional team members, trust, and cooperation

Developing and implementing protection programs for families is different than doing so for corporate clients. Programs in corporate environments are structured, managed and delivered in keeping with corporate practices. Processes are formalized in ways similar to other business practices; decisions are made according to well-defined criteria; hierarchies are pretty clear.

Families are different. Emotions, feelings, and personal relations matter in a different way, as do self-image and perceptions. That's not good or bad; that's just the reality of working in the context of the family. And security professionals need to get it.

Family programs must view all family members as principals – from the spouse to children, parents and even friends. The important thing to understand here is that protection teams will be addressing different cultures, sets of expectations, and financial arrangements – and that everything must be customized to match the family's preferences, not a corporation's.

Key differences concern family dynamics and planning. Family programs must generally be more flexible than corporate, more sensitive to emotional needs, and even more able to adapt quickly to changing plans. Team members need to be comfortable with even more gray areas and potentially less communication and information. Even more than in corporate environments, this requires team members that have rock-solid judgment, creative problem-solving skills, and good intuition. They need to be people who like working with and for other people – in addition to being tactically competent.

Trust is earned by sharing information – and respecting confidentiality

The importance of developing strong, trusting relationships throughout the family ecosystem cannot be over emphasized. Everyone delivering support to the family, whether on the security team, in estate management, or the family office will have different levels of communication and kinds of interaction with family members. Sharing information, lessons learned and best practices across these groups goes a long way to establishing security program success.

But information sharing comes with responsibility and requires a mature understanding of confidentiality. Everyone serving the family in one capacity or another has access to different types of information. Some in the ecosystem should and do have more access to family members than others, and information is often compartmentalized for a reason. Sensitivities about what should be shared with whom and when are critical.

The goal for the team is to develop trust with the family members and each other. There may be times when one group or person has more trust from the family members and will want to solidify their position with the family by not sharing information that should be shared with other parts of the ecosystem. This can set up power struggles that are frustrating and destructive – and never add value for the family or its protection. Professional managers are aware of this potentiality and work hard to create a team environment across the family ecosystem. Choosing team members and leaders that have mature interpersonal skills and can keep their egos in check is a critical element in hiring.

4. Get ready for changes in the ecosystem and evolving client needs – and make sure programs are ready to adapt

Finally, no matter how hard we work to establish a great family protection program, we must face the fact that this, too, will change.

Babies are born. Young adults go off to college and new jobs. Personal relationships begin, evolve, and end. Staff are hired and fired, or move on for many reasons, too. And yes, the risks, threats and vulnerabilities that inform security measures are also ever-changing.

Successful family protection programs take a proactive approach to these dynamics. They focus on ongoing quality control and HR development, develop ways to combat team complacency and boost responsiveness to client needs.

Chapter 5:
Secure travel support for high net worth families

Why high net worth families need secure travel support: Prominence and wealth increase the risks

The lifestyles of high net worth families often include lots of travel, both domestically and abroad. In addition to the risks that all travelers face, however, from the banal but all-too-common traffic accident to getting mugged in an unfamiliar city, the prominence and wealth of high net worth individuals call for extra caution and care, as well as special measures to ensure their privacy.

Prominence makes it more difficult to fly under the public radar. Curious passersby ask for autographs and handouts. Paparazzi are always on the prowl. Itineraries and agendas get leaked from any number of sources. Bored taxi or limo drivers might send a "look who I'm driving with" to their friends. And the ubiquitous use of social media, also by high net worth individuals themselves, can easily broadcast whereabouts, plans and other personal details.

Furthermore, wealth increases the likelihood of crimes ranging from shakedowns to break-ins and kidnappings. Unfortunately, this holds true for parents as well as children, whether it's young children traveling with nannies or teens, or students traveling on their own.

Another important reason the high net worth professionals and families seek out specialized secure travel support is productivity. Staying connected through 24/7 online access is only one way this happens. Just as important is the extra time available when you're not the one who has to drive the car but can work or relax while moving through traffic from one meeting to the next – or from one tourist destination to another.

High net worth individuals and families are used to a high degree of customized support in other areas of their lives, so it's no wonder they increasingly want the same kind of customization when it comes to their secure travel needs. Let's look at some of the options.

What kinds of secure travel support do the high net worth individuals and families need and get

Customized secure ground travel is the missing link between business- or first-class air travel, high-end hotels and all the other places the C-suite needs to visit. The same holds true for high net worth families and individuals.

So, for starters, let's compare how secure travel support stacks up against the alternatives.

Secure travel comparison	Low-end	Mid-range	High-end (Secure travel support)
Airport pickup	None	Driver waiting with Family name on a placard or iPad	Driver waiting with code name on a placard or iPad; telephone arrangement
Ground transportation from airport to hotel, around town, etc.	Taxi, Uber or public transportation	Driver or limo service	Security driver and vehicle
Driver trained in security driving	No	No	Yes
Driver vetted by security professionals	No	Maybe	Yes
GPS traveler tracking	No	No	Yes, if desired
Driver prepped on itinerary to know best and alternative routes, best drop-off and pick-up locations	No	Maybe	Yes
Local police escorts in high-risk areas	No	No	Yes, if required and available
In-car amenities: water, soft drinks, snacks, etc.	Rarely	Maybe	Always – and according to family brief

Secure travel comparison	Low-end	Mid-range	High-end (Secure travel support)
In-car wifi	No	No	Yes
Hotel			
Security pre-check of hotel	No	No	Yes
Hotel check-in	Wait in line at reception; check in with own name	Wait in line at reception; check in with own name	Pre-check -in under alias; go directly to room
Payment	Own credit card	Own credit card	Anonymous credit card
Travel intel and family protection			
Intelligence updates on country and local travel risks	No	No	Yes
Close protection as needed	No	No	Yes
Advance work to secure local travel itinerary	No	No	Yes

Secure travel comparison	Low-end	Mid-range	High-end (Secure travel support)
Emergency response and operations center back-up			
Project manager/ops center available for crisis management, problem solving and to advise client on logistics efficiencies and security developments	No	No	Yes, 24/7 Operations Center back-up
Operations center can arrange other transportation on the fly (charter jets, helicopters, commercial flights)	No	No	Yes

As you can see in the table above, high-end secure travel support adds an extra layer of safety at every step of the way. It's not that all high-end travelers check off every box in the right-hand column for every trip. That will depend on travel itineraries as well as personal circumstances and preferences. Vetted and well-trained security drivers are normally a good starting point that provide many important benefits. Other services can be added as needs evolve.

Let's have a closer look at some of the things that make high-end secure travel support different.

Security drivers: The use of security drivers is usually the first way that high net worth individuals and families improve their peace of mind while on the road.

Yes, terrorist attacks and other headline-grabbing events cause concern. But the single largest cause of fatalities for travelers is still traffic accidents. The WHO counts these in "road fatalities per 100,000 vehicles", and the spread between countries is significant. The U.S. reports 12.9. Most Western European countries and Japan are in the single digits. China clocks in at 104, India 130, Nigeria 615. You get the picture.

While no driver can completely eradicate the possibility of a traffic accident, carefully selected security drivers significantly mitigate the risk and reduce the probability.

For one thing, these drivers and their vehicles are vetted against a variety of criteria by professionals with international experience. Where possible and legal to do so, they check on a variety of critical factors that may include driver backgrounds, criminal and traffic records, specialized training, and more. They also ensure that vehicles live up to objective safety and comfort standards.

For another, confidentiality clauses and individual non-disclosure agreements (NDAs) are built into contracts. This ensures that drivers know the importance of maintaining the anonymity of their passengers and that sanctions are applied if confidentiality is violated. This is much less likely to occur when the companies providing secure drivers have long-term, ongoing relationships with either the client or the company representing them.

Most limo drivers are primarily concerned with comfort and convenience – but are not trained in the security aspects of driving such as looking out for potential threats, defensive and evasive driving tactics, etc. Vetted security drivers are different.

Global security operations centers: Global security centers (GSOCs) provide a one-stop, 24/7 hub of communication, connectivity, travel and other intelligence, and emergency back-up services for travelers and those they need to stay in touch with. While many corporate clients are familiar with GSOCs in connection with executive protection for their C-suites, this may not be the case for high net worth individuals and families.

Depending on client needs and preferences, GSOC services can include:

- Traveler tracking via secured GPS devices

- Daily reports on traveler movements and locations to executive administrative assistants or family members

- 24/7 responsiveness and, in case of emergencies, including the rapid deployment of local resources as needed

- Communication with the traveler to ensure that travelers stay connected/are reachable as needed

- Travel intelligence in the form of daily reports on locations regarding general threats and risks, emerging or acute threats, specific threats connected to principals such as persons or groups of interest, and more

Executive protection agents: Executive protection agents, also known as "close protection agents", bring an extra dimension of security for travelers. This can include:

- ***Advances:*** Checking itinerary venues to assess risk prior to the arrival of the principal – and recommending or making necessary adjustments

- ***Close protection:*** Providing close protection while the individual goes about his or her business, or the family is out enjoying themselves

- ***When the family is driving:*** The agent can do this either by traveling alongside them or behind them in a separate vehicle

- ***Hotel check-ins:*** Checking into hotels for principals to increase anonymity, reduce their visibility and save them time

- ***Local fixer:*** Making sure the principals get done what they need while in unfamiliar settings, from taking care of forgotten meds to getting into restaurants. This function can be especially valuable in emerging markets where knowing how things work locally – and who to call – can make a big difference

Contrary to popular stereotypes, good executive protection agents know how to blend in unobtrusively and only stand out when necessary. Should the individual or family require even more discretion, covert protection and surveillance detection are also possibilities. These services create even more distance between agents and principals but have the same goal: to stop threats as quickly and as far away from the principal as possible.

Why it's helpful to use a specialist partner for secure travel support

Few families have the resources, networks, or time to find

security drivers and executive protection agents around the world. Instead, they rely on trusted specialist partners for:

- Direct access to proven drivers and protection agents in multiple locations

- Consistent, ongoing vetting to ensure security, quality and reliability against agreed standards

- Negotiating fair prices in different markets

The convenience of "one-stop shopping", no matter when or where the travelers' itineraries take them, is one reason to engage a specialist partner for secure travel services. The peace of mind that you've done what you can to protect loved ones is another.

Chapter 6:
Licensing and legal compliance issues in protective security: What high net worth families need to know

There is a lot of confusion surrounding licensing and legal compliance issues concerning private security services, including the protective services relevant for high net worth families. The problems are complex, and there are plenty of gray areas open to interpretation. The laws that impact non-governmental security services all vary considerably from country to country and even within one country. And even though the security consequences of good or bad training are significant, training requirements vary wildly from one place to another.

In the United States, for example, the regulation of private security is left up to the states and not to the federal government. Some states have no regulation of civilian security services whatsoever; others maintain complex sets of legislation. Training standards, criminal record checking, licensing, and oversight all change at the state line – even though the nature of relevant threats and the basics of good protective security remain largely the same.

Countries, states, and municipalities organize the regulation of private security in a hodgepodge of different ways. In Florida, the installation of security alarms is controlled by the Department of Business and Professional Regulation while anything having to do with security personnel or investigations comes under the aegis of the Department of Agriculture and Consumer Services' Division of Licensing. In Ireland, the Private Security Authority regulates everything the private security industry does. In Italy and France, various police agencies, national, and departmental authorities are all involved in controlling private security services.

The law of unintended consequences: How efforts to mitigate security risks can open new risks of legal liability

To avoid liability, you need to know precisely what is required and allowed in every different jurisdiction, and how regulations impact specific security services in specific contexts. What is legal in one place might not be in another. What is good, acceptable practice in one situation might expose you to legal risks and civil suits in another.

We know of cases where major corporations have hired experienced protective security professionals with stellar backgrounds in military or government services but didn't think to check local licensing requirements. Guess what? The corporations were noncompliant and were thus liable to fines and civil suits. Even though the protective agents are highly trained pros, they can't protect the CEO unless they have taken a few hours of superficial training to become properly licensed locally.

We know of other cases where high net worth families hire their own security personnel (armed or unarmed) for residential protection – even though these families have no professional experience regarding labor laws or security, standard operating procedures, protective training, or best practices. Whether such programs actually mitigate security risks is one question. Whether they mitigate or increase liability risks is another: If you don't run the show properly, it's still your show.

Depending on local legislation, such direct hires may not need to be licensed or have any formal training at all. But they may not be able to conduct security anywhere but on the family's property, either. As soon as they step onto the sidewalk – off private property and into a public space – their activities come under the jurisdiction of the state and they can no longer legally perform any kind of protective intervention. If protective personnel do not consistently make razor-sharp distinctions between being on private or public property when working for families, they expose their employers to significant liability if anything goes wrong – or if any lawyer gets interested for the wrong reasons.

Hiring off-duty police for private security is not always as simple as it seems

Some families hire off-duty police for residential protection and expect that everything will be fine. Police have security experience, of course, and they also have strong networks they can call if the need arises. Now don't get us wrong: We've got nothing but respect for the men and women working in law enforcement, and many of our colleagues in the security industry have paid their dues in the public sector before joining the private sector. But the duties and approaches of police officers differ fundamentally from those of executive and residential protection personnel.

For one thing, police work is generally reactive – responding to incidents after the fact – whereas the focus of private protection work is generally proactive and attempts to prevent incidents from happening. Proper training for both professions differs accordingly.

For another, licensing requirements are not the same. In California, for example, everyone performing private security services (including retired and off-duty law enforcement officers) must be registered with the state's Bureau of Security and Investigative Services – something law enforcement officers and their private employers don't always realize or comply with.

Employing public servants in private settings raises other issues, too – some obvious to high net worth families, some less so. Staffing can be a problem, as "the day job" will always be prioritized when there is a scheduling conflict or sudden change of plans. It's readily apparent that people who work full-time in one job are hardly fresh and well rested when they start their moonlight shift. But there are also ambiguities concerning the legal liabilities of off-duty police working in private security that families don't always appreciate.

Police officers are generally sworn to enforce the law 24/7, whether they are on duty or not. In some jurisdictions, officers are required by law to carry a weapon while they are off-duty; in others, they are not. How are off-duty police officers supposed to respond in an emergency if their law enforcement oath is at odds with their private client's security needs? Can they run a suspicious car's license plate number when they're on a protective security job? What if they notice something illegal happening on the street while working on a client's property – are they obligated to leave their private job to perform their public duty, or exonerated if they don't? Is it OK to arrest someone for harassing a client, even though such behavior may not be considered a crime or misdemeanor in court? Do they need to identify themselves as police officers if they intervene while working for a private client? Who is liable if an off-duty police officer's actions become the object of a civil court case – the officer, the department, or the employer?

We could go on, but we think you get the point: Families need to consider their exposure to liabilities carefully – even when this includes off-duty police officers.

Security services are always regulated for a reason. But how they're regulated isn't always reasonable

Police everywhere are tasked with protecting people and property and upholding the law. As representatives of the state, they have what sociologists call the "monopoly on the legitimate use of physical force": Only the police are allowed to use force against fellow citizens. We willingly accept this tradeoff – giving up our right to use force in return for general lawfulness and security – because it works out well for everyone when it's based on legitimate ways of doing things.

Private security services are generally seen as a supplement to state actors such as police forces. They provide security that is additional to what the police provide, but they don't replace the police, or, in general, take part in the police's monopoly of the use of force. This is an important distinction that forms the basis of the myriad ways different governmental bodies relate to private security services. How can legislators ensure that people can satisfy their needs for enhanced security without undermining the state's monopoly of the use of force? The answer is regulation.

Governments around the world regulate private security companies in one way or another. Regulation can include everything from codes of conduct to use of force, use of weapons, minimum training standards, transparency of police records, information sharing, uniforms and more.

If all governments regulated security in a similar fashion, our lives in the security industry would be easier and the regulatory pitfalls that face families hiring security services would be more predictable and easier to avoid. The problem is, governments regulate security in very different ways. Some ways work better than others. Frankly, some don't work well at all.

According to a report by the United Nations, states fall into three broad categories when it comes to regulation of private security services. In UN-speak, a "state" is a member country; for our purposes, the term applies just as well to countries and individual states within the U.S. or other legislative entities in other countries. The UN defines these three categories as:

- States with no regulation

- States with inadequate regulation

- States with effective regulation

According to the authors of the report, "Most states fall into the first two categories".

Based on our professional experience across the U.S. and in many countries around the world, we can only agree. The regulation of private security services is uneven at best. At worst, state regulations, which stipulate only minimum requirements, can give a false sense of security and open new dimensions of liability and risk.

Licensed security personnel: What does that even mean?

It is important to understand the scope and limitations of state regulations concerning security. Take licensing, for example. Occupational licensing is common for professions that can have significant negative effects on people – think of medicine, law or structural engineering – so states set up licensing requirements to protect their citizens (and to protect professions, of course.) But states also have licensing requirements for all kinds of other lines of work, from plumbers to morticians. Most states require security personnel to be licensed, too.

Licensing criteria for security include things like age, training and background checks. Internationally, some countries do a decent job, for example, Israel, South Africa and the UK. Most countries have minimal licensing standards that inspire minimal confidence.

Within the U.S., licensing requirements vary wildly from state to state. The good news is that most U.S. states (41) do, in fact, require security personnel to be licensed and thus live up to a set of minimum standards. The bad news is these standards fluctuate so broadly that they are impossible to compare – and that "minimum requirements" can be so minimal that they are basically worthless.

Seven U.S. states require no background checks of security officers at all, and only three have set up reliable programs that utilize FBI data to run in-depth, country-wide security checks even though this is possible under federal law.

Some U.S. states require security personnel to undergo a relatively respectable, but in our opinion unimpressive, 40 hours of training as a minimum. Most ask for far less. Some stipulate annual refresher courses, most don't. Nine states have no regulations for security personnel at all. Over 20 states require no training of unarmed security at all. South Carolina mandates a grand total of four hours of training to become a licensed security officer, then another four hours to be licensed as an armed security officer. Compare this to South Carolina's minimum training requirements of 300 hours to become a licensed manicurist, and you begin to get a sense of how arbitrary and ineffective regulatory requirements can be.

Legislative attempts to tighten up regulation get stranded for all kinds of reasons. Anti-regulatory sentiment in many places prevents new laws that create new restrictions. Both large security firms and mom-and-pop operations lobby against tighter regulations that would force them to spend more money on training. State agencies balk at legislation that would require better background checks since this would incur more costs for them.

So, what's a family to do?

Rather than blindly depend on state governments to set standards that are reliable and effective, high net worth families should be aware of the actual requirements that must be fulfilled for licensing where they live and work – then be prepared to go beyond them.

One might doubt that most high net worth families, upon careful consideration of all the facts, would decide that hiring the cheapest licensed security provider or a few off-duty police officers is the answer to all their needs and wishes. But we see this happen all the time.

Instead, we believe that families need to set their own standards. This is admittedly not a simple thing to do, so most families choose to work with specialist partners to define the criteria that should inform the design of protective programs and then implement them.

We encourage high net worth families to use the same types of criteria that states expect security companies to meet, but to go beyond minimum standards to source vendors and programs that actually work.

These criteria should as a minimum include:

Sufficient initial and ongoing training in a variety of security skills and additional training in firearm use if relevant. The minimum requirements stipulated by most U.S. states and many countries are far from adequate in our experience. There are other and higher national standards, however, which point in the right direction. Israel requires up to three months training for executive protection personnel; South Africa's Private Security Industry Regulatory Authority maintains a detailed set of robust training requirements for a wide range of security functions; the UK's Security Industry Authority requires a minimum of 140 hours, which we think is a reasonable minimum requirement for executive protection positions, while at least 80 hours should be demanded for entry-level residential security positions. And don't forget continuing training to keep perishable skills fresh.

Extensive pre-employment and ongoing background checks that reliably reveal candidates with criminal records and other pertinent issues. In the U.S., this means more than the superficial background checks that are commercially available. Does the protective security candidate have a history of litigation? Has he or she sued previous employers? What about personal debt and collection accounts? Someone could meet all the criminal criteria but still have cash flow problems that make working with a prominent family, with millions in jewels and cash, an unfortunate incident waiting to happen. If the family does not have the means to perform sufficient background checks, they should work with a reliable partner who does.

Quality assurance methods that hold personnel and programs accountable to measurable standards and proactively combat complacency. If security providers can't demonstrate how they maintain program quality, they probably aren't. Families have the right to know how they can determine the readiness of their protective team to prevent security breaches and respond to incidents if necessary. After all, just because nothing usually happens doesn't necessarily mean that the team is competent.

Full liability insurance for all protective personnel including workers' compensation, general liability, and professional liability policies. It's important that families understand all insurance issues – whether they hire security personnel directly or through a third party.

Families don't need to have all the answers, but asking the right questions and comparing how alternative security providers respond to them will go a long way.

Chapter 7:
The role of intelligence analysis in high net worth protection programs

The practice of intelligence analysis originated in national intelligence agencies tasked with supporting national security, foreign policy, and military objectives, and used to be something that only governments took seriously.

However, intelligence analysts now play an increasingly important role in safeguarding a wide variety of corporate interests, too, ranging from the protection of people to understanding risks that might impact anything from supply chains to critical assets such as production facilities, brands and reputations.

We believe the time has come to broaden the purview of intelligence analysts to include the protection of high net worth individuals and families. We are already using this in many of our programs, and we are convinced that as the complexity of risk mitigation increases, intelligence analysis will prove its worth in even more.

What is intelligence analysis?

Simply put, intelligence analysis is a process that mitigates risk and enables more informed decisions by a better understanding of complex and often ambiguous situations.

The classical process used by intelligence analysts comprises the continuing refinement of data (unorganized, unrelated bits of facts) into information (data that is organized to be meaningful and useful, for example, by answering questions such as "who, what, when, where…"). And, finally this information can be translated into intelligence, which, for our purposes, we define as actionable insights for decision making about risk mitigation.

Intelligence analysts are not the ones who make decisions or offer recommendations. Rather, they support other stakeholders and decision makers by the process of refinement described above in order to constantly monitor and understand the many contexts relevant to security objectives. They do this primarily by preparing a variety of reports, both regular and ad hoc, on topics that impact security and risk mitigation. These reports can include topics ranging from persons of interest, evolving trends, or assessments of acute developments and major incidents.

How and where is intelligence analysis a relevant part of high net worth protection?

Solid intelligence is at the heart of any good protective program. Indeed, intelligence is what informs the Risk, Threat, and Vulnerability Analysis (RTVA) that form the foundation of solid protective work – and all protective programs should be intelligence based.

Intelligence analysis performed by experienced and well-managed intelligence analysts adds value to high net worth protection programs in a variety of ways. Let's examine how.

The importance of prominence, offline...

To begin with, intelligence analysis forms part of a proactive approach to understanding how the prominence of the principal and his or her family impacts their risks, threats and vulnerabilities. Understanding the degree of relative prominence, and what drives that prominence, is critical. As was established in the Secret Service's Exceptional Case Study[4], increased prominence levels correlate with increased risk for public figures and celebrities, and the actual perpetrators of attacks are not easily identifiable due to demographic markers or obvious stalking patterns.

Intelligence analysis can be a powerful way to identify and understand the threats facing the principal and family, as well as the individuals, environments, and sentiments that might play a critical role in risk mitigation. This includes, but is not limited to, keeping track of persons of interest and groups of interest. Effective intel allows the security apparatus to proactively prepare measures to prevent negative activity, keep abreast of

---

[4] See https://www.secretservice.gov/protection/ntac/research/

(and share internally) negative messages with regard to the principal's reputation and assess the current sentiment around the principal and the family.

...and online

A key piece of the intelligence analysis puzzle is identifying and assessing what information is available online regarding the principal and family members.

Social media behavior might in some cases tip off later violent behavior, and social listening can be an effective way to identify isolated threats as well as evolving threat patterns. Lone actors who perpetrate mass shootings are sometimes found to have left trails of clues and threats of violence on social media – unfortunately and far too often after the fact.

But intelligence analysts can also discover and report other pertinent information online. What is being shared that creates more time and place predictability, controversy, or potential access? If there is time and place predictability, what can be done to reduce the risks involved? A well-run intel program informs the people responsible for security of their findings to enable pre-emptive countermeasures throughout the family ecosystem.

Intelligence and location, location, location

Intelligence analysts can also help us to understand location-based threats that impact family members, be they related to primary or other residences, schools, workplaces, or travel destinations.

Residential intelligence: Intelligence analysis – both the kind performed by trained intelligence analysts and the kind performed by experienced protection agents – is an important part of residential security. We need to understand all the different communities the principal might call home, including where the primary residence is located, as well as any second, third or other residences – or yacht moorings, for that matter.

Good residential intelligence can take on many forms. It can be as simple as maintaining good relationships between neighbors and protective agents. We all share a mutual interest in keeping the neighborhood safe, so cooperating with neighbors to share information on what's happening nearby is essential. As in many other aspects of life, we need to understand that to give is to get. When protective agents, who often have access to other kinds of information on local happenings than local residents, judiciously share intel that can help the neighbors stay safe, happy and productive, then neighbors are more likely to share what they learn that is relevant to neighborhood security.

Protective agents are also an important part of the intelligence team. They converse with neighbors, passersby and the postman. They are on the ground and play an important role in surveillance and counter surveillance. Like analysts, they need to have a proven way of passing on the intelligence they gather so that it can be useful for better decisions. And they should always maintain a customer service mindset that also extends to the neighbors – and try to benefit the neighborhood, too.

The same goes for working with local police, with whom close cooperation is essential in both preventing and responding to security incidents.

Finally, as we all know, social media groups with community focus are also a good way to keep up-to-date on what's happening locally. Yes, these sources might include more information than you want on canine excrement, but they can also provide valuable information on local politics, cultural activities, current events, suspicious types and other topics that might affect residential security in the short and long terms.

Travel intelligence: Intelligence on destinations is an essential way to prepare for travel. This can be facilitated by general travel risk advisories such as those provided in English by the United States, the United Kingdom or Australia.

The U.S. State Department's Overseas Security Advisory Council (OSAC) provides even more granular and updated travel advisories. Especially OSAC's "Crime and Safety Reports" and "Analyses" provide information that is helpful, detailed and timely.

But experienced intelligence analysts dig even deeper. For one thing, they will probably have access to commercial incident reporting tools, including those sold by vendors such as Risk Line, Dataminr, and Stabilitas, so they get immediate updates on incidents as they occur in locations where the principal or family is traveling. For another, they will often have their own network of on-the-ground resources. These local eyes and ears can be invaluable in sourcing near-real-time information on everything from demonstrations on the street to road closings to labor unrest and more – all of which might be relevant to the itineraries and safety of travelers.

Reputation protection is a key function of intelligence analysis

Intelligence analysts also play an important role in protecting the reputations of their principals. They do this by monitoring social media and other online sources for any mention of the principal and family members, but also by keeping tabs on other keywords that are relevant to the principal's privacy and security – both on- and offline.

While the primary focus of reputation protection will usually be privacy, the security benefits are also critical. Prominent people also make conspicuous targets for theft of personal data, blackmail, corporate and personal espionage, and more.

Monitoring of the principal and family's on- and offline reputation should also include any public mention of the principal's security program, which can be a double-edged sword. On the one hand, the awareness that the principal indeed does benefit from residential and other protective services can be a deterrent that prevents some from attempting to breach security. On the other hand, however, media coverage of security efforts may compromise operational integrity. In either case, protection managers need to know this information in order to take their precautions.

Vetting, investigations and data protection: Essential but sensitive tasks

Finally, it should be mentioned that intelligence analysts can be of significant assistance in vetting candidates for job openings in family offices, including portfolio managers, grounds keepers and everything in between, and in investigating incidents.

But while we all naturally turn to the internet to research people, there are legal pitfalls that employers need to be aware of. For example, unless the organization has a clear written policy regarding the kinds of on- and offline information that may be used, how it will be gathered and stored and by whom, the family office might make itself liable to discriminatory practices or other violations of privacy and/or labor laws.

Intelligence analysts can provide an arm's length distance between the vetting of candidates by trained research professionals, and the hiring managers who use vetted shortlists to decide between qualified candidates.

Individual family offices often do not possess the same resources as corporations, and this can be a disadvantage in terms of compliance. For example, all corporations that do business in the European Union are (or should be!) fully aware of the EU's General Data Protection Regulation, which lays down strict rules on how personal data is collected, stored and protected and came into effect on May 28, 2018. Families with residences and employees within the EU can easily expose themselves to liabilities if they are not in compliance.

How successful high net worth security programs integrate intelligence analysis

To our knowledge, family offices with experience in setting up any kind of intelligence analysis program are few and far between. While some families may initially rely on the principal's corporate intelligence program for personal and family coverage, this often entails the potential for confusion about who is paying for what and is not sustainable long term. Instead, high net worth individuals and families who want the benefits of dedicated intelligence analysis support usually turn to specialist partners.

Intelligence analysts employed by specialist partners provide a number of advantages. To begin with, they have experience in hiring, developing and retaining the particular talent required for success – something those responsible for HR in the family office most likely do not.

Furthermore, they are more likely to provide an accessible network of other intelligence analysts, both those working for the specialist partner and others. Such communities of practice are essential. They broaden the geographical reach of any analyst, providing the kinds of on-the-ground intel described above; they provide broad access to deep pockets of domain expertise in case this is needed; and they provide the learning opportunities that help intelligence analysts thrive personally and professionally.

Finally, specialist partners provide scalability so that intelligence programs can quickly ramp up or down according to the family office's evolving needs. For many, a fractional solution with less than one full-time analyst assigned may be the best way to begin. These outsourced but dedicated resources can be increased if necessary, or quickly terminated if they prove, against expectations, to be ineffective.

Part II:
Managing family protective security programs

Introduction to Part II

Part II of our book deals with the management of protective programs for high net worth individuals and families.

We begin Part II with the story of Tom, a new security manager with a stellar background but no experience working with private families. We believe Tom's story illustrates the importance of adjusting protective practices learned elsewhere – for example, in government, military or corporate contexts – to the realities of working in the intimate environment of home and family.

Although we've made this cautionary tale anonymous, we base it on real experience. While this particular story does not end well for Tom, we hope it will drive home the point that the protective security industry is all about people. Neither principals nor family offices new to the game know exactly what they are looking for in a security director or security agents and discover this incrementally by finding out what they are NOT looking for. Everyone from the newest residential agent to the security director can enjoy the principal's good graces one minute and be out of a job the next. We hope security managers

– as well as those responsible for managing them – will remember Tom's story as they read the subsequent chapters of Part II.

As we see in Chapter 8, the first responsibility of the family protective security manager is to define program objectives that are specific, actionable, and measurable, and that fit the family's needs now. That mitigating risk in accordance with best industry practices is important will surprise no one. But we are often surprised that another key objective, aligning the protective program with family culture and personal preferences, does not get the management focus that it deserves.

Chapters 9, 10 and 11 answer some of the most common questions family offices have about protective roles, qualifications, and staffing levels. Chapter 9 reviews the required skills and prerequisite training most commonly needed in family protective programs. Chapter 10 outlines the primary roles in protective teams. And Chapter 11 provides some guidelines for determining how to dimension and staff programs.

Chapter 12 focuses on the security manager's all-important role in motivating team members and ensuring smooth communication within the team as well as between the team and other stakeholders.

In Chapter 13, we introduce key performance indicators (KPIs) for family security programs. While specific KPIs will vary by program, of course, we believe this general introduction to the topic will help families and family offices – as well as practitioners new to the field – to understand the importance of getting specific in defining what constitutes good performance, and consistently following up on security teams to ensure that they deliver as agreed.

Recruiting and developing great employees are prerequisites for any organization's success. In Chapter 14, we share our experience in these vital HR tasks as they apply to high net worth security.

Finally, we close Part II with two chapters on procurement issues. In Chapter 15, we present some considerations regarding the make-buy decision. Assuming many family offices will eventually ask a handful of potential vendors to submit how they would supply security services, Chapter 16 describes how to write an RFP.

The story of Tom

Tom was the new security director for a very prominent family. He had never worked in the private sector before and landed the job not least because of a resume that included a long stint in the United States Secret Service. Tom was a gifted protector and was extremely knowledgeable in many areas. He looked the part, too, and had all the qualities the family office thought would be necessary to run the family's security and protection program.

In Tom's mind, security was the single most important thing for the principals. They had hired him specifically to create and run a protective program for the family, and conversations with the principals had made it clear that they were all on the same page regarding key security objectives. What Tom didn't realize in his early days of an exciting new job was that he needed to consider his position as security director in a context that was very different than what he had been used to, one that included family dynamics and interpersonal relationships that had played no role in his previous career with the government.

The family had a head housekeeper, Molly, whom they really loved. Molly had worked for the family for more than ten years, starting out way before the family's growing prominence made enhanced security a necessity. The principals and their children considered Molly a part of the family, and the feeling was mutual.

Molly had earned the family's confidence and was tasked with a lot. Her days were busy planning and seeing through many of the day-to-day jobs that kept the estate running. The security agents that worked the front gate were used to seeing Molly come and go and were always quick to buzz her back in when she approached the gatehouse.

A few weeks into his new role as security director, Tom was tightening up some standard operating procedures and working with his staff at the gate. Molly rolled up and gave her usual toot on the horn to let the agents know it was her. Tom eyed a learning opportunity and made the point to his team that they needed to visually verify everyone before letting them in, regardless of how many times they entered or exited the estate. He didn't buzz Molly in, but instead required that she back up her vehicle to the camera and roll her window down.

Now, up until this point, one could argue that Tom was in the right. He was training his security team on standard operating procedures, all of which are critical to maintaining effective security, and he needed to be sure that these protocols were understood and routinely followed not only by his agents, but by everyone who worked at the estate.

There are lots of ways to get things done. Tom's didn't take into consideration the importance of understanding the culture of his new workplace. Molly was visibly frustrated and said, "Tom, please let me in. You know who I am. Your guys know who I am. I need to get in".

Tom didn't like her tone or the inference that she felt disrespected. Instead of defusing the situation with some verbal charm, he barked back at her and said, "And you know who I am. I'm the director of security, and I'm making changes to how things are run around here. This isn't your house, Molly". The conversation escalated further. Tom explained his role, flashed his career experience, and did a little chest thumping. Who knew how to run security, Tom or Molly? In the end, Tom let her onto the property, but she was upset and embarrassed by the whole situation, and how aggressively Tom had talked down to her.

Once Molly had a bad taste in her mouth from her interactions with Tom, she started to ask other estate staff about their experiences. The gardeners also expressed concern with how Tom talked to them; they were not alone.

Later that week, the principals ran into Molly in the residence and checked in with her as they normally do. They asked Molly how things were going, what was new, and what she thought of the new security director. Molly shared exactly what she thought of Tom: Someone that threw his weight and title around, was arrogant, and treated staff and visitors rudely, as if he was some sort of prison guard. Of course, Tom had no idea that Molly had the principals' ears or that they relied on her for information. If he had, he may have treated her more kindly. In any case, he could have treated everyone equally and with the same respect.

Shortly thereafter, Tom was let go.

The principals didn't like his demeanor when dealing with the estate's staff and visitors. Yes, they understood that security was important, but they didn't want their residence to feel like a prison. Tom's lack of emotional intelligence reflected negatively on the principals whom he represented. His actions had direct consequences on how they were perceived and how they perceived themselves. The estate was their sanctuary, and they wanted it to feel like a home, not a corporate campus.

The principals were more active in hiring their next security director. They used the recruitment and interview process to evaluate the cultural fit of all the candidates, eager to find someone who covered the security base but would also integrate well with the family and staff and promote the peaceful nature of the home which they treasured so highly.

The protective security industry is all about people. Everyone from the newest residential agent to the security director can enjoy the principal's good graces one minute and be out of a job the next. We've made our own fair share of mistakes and have learned the importance of cultural fit the hard way.

In our experience, a security director has 100 days to make a positive or negative impression with the principals. Tom didn't last 100 days. It's common that principals new to the game do not know exactly what they are looking for in a security director or security agents and discover this incrementally by finding out what they are NOT looking for. Better advice during the recruitment of new personnel definitely helps. But ultimately, it's up to the principal to decide whom they enjoy working with and whom they don't.

Chapter 8:
Setting objectives for the family security program

The overarching purpose of a family security program can be boiled down to a simple idea: mitigating risk to the family members to an acceptable level.

While such a broad statement of purpose might be a good description of a family security program's overall protection objectives, however, the goal is too broad to guide the managers who are responsible for actually making this happen in any practical way.

What is an acceptable risk level? Why is it acceptable? According to which criteria? What if we spent twice as much money? What can we learn from benchmarking with other families in similar situations and with similar needs?

Of course, the answers to these questions will always depend on an in-depth analysis of the family's situation and should only be answered once there is a good understanding of the actual risks, threats and vulnerabilities – and the family's personal preferences.

All protective programs, from the most basic to the most complex, depend on layers of security to make sure any hostile activity is deterred as far from the principals as possible and as quickly as possible. How these security layers are set up and maintained varies widely according to program complexity and maturity, and the family's evolving needs.

The range of protective coverage evolves with the family's needs

Most residential security programs start with something as simple as an alarm system for their principal residence. Initially, most of these are off-the-shelf solutions from alarm companies, and only later do most families opt for more sophisticated, personalized solutions. Programs typically evolve from there to include residential security agents, at first part-time, then full-time. A next step could be security drivers for the principals or other family members. From there, close protection agents might be added for one or more family members, in one or more situations, e.g., at work, at school, while at events, etc.

Some families require even more coverage. As babies are born, young children begin exploring the world, and older children move off to college, program needs change. Surveillance protection agents and covert protection agents strengthen security layers in a discreet way. Additional coverage for secondary residences might be required, as might security for planes or yachts. Philanthropic activities might necessitate separate but coordinated security programs.

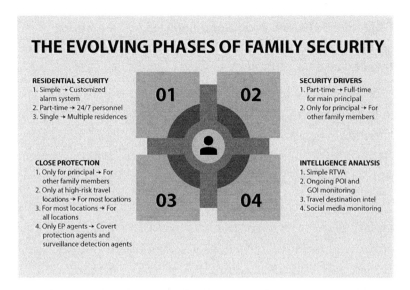

THE EVOLVING PHASES OF FAMILY SECURITY

RESIDENTIAL SECURITY
1. Simple → Customized alarm system
2. Part-time → 24/7 personnel
3. Single → Multiple residences

01

02

SECURITY DRIVERS
1. Part-time → Full-time for main principal
2. Only for principal → For other family members

CLOSE PROTECTION
1. Only for principal → For other family members
2. Only at high-risk travel locations → For most locations
3. For most locations → For all locations
4. Only EP agents → Covert protection agents and surveillance detection agents

03

04

INTELLIGENCE ANALYSIS
1. Simple RTVA
2. Ongoing POI and GOI monitoring
3. Travel destination intel
4. Social media monitoring

Whatever the objectives, budgets are always a constraint.

The first responsibility of the family protective security manager is to define program objectives that are specific, actionable, and measurable - and that fit the family's needs now. These goals must be clear to the family protection team, the principals and all key players in the family ecosystem – and accepted by all. Even when these goals pull in different directions, good family security managers find creative ways to strike a consistent, high-performing equilibrium among them. We need to define what success looks like, achieve consensus on this vision of success from the principals and staff, then design operations that deliver on these success criteria – and to stay on track, follow up relentlessly on how we perform.

In this chapter, we propose three overall objectives that apply to practically any family protection program, no matter how complex or mature it is. Specific program objectives should then build on and expand these high-level goals.

Objective 1: Match program deliveries to an ongoing analysis of the principal's profile and the resulting risks, threats, and vulnerabilities

Whether they like it or not, high net worth individuals and their families are often public figures who get a lot of media attention. Their prominence can, in fact, be higher than politicians or celebrities with significant name recognition – people with whom they would never compare themselves otherwise.

Family protection programs must consider the principal's profile, as well as any events or changes that could impact that profile when setting objectives. It is important that the Risk, Threat, and Vulnerability Analysis (RTVA) we introduced in Part I is not a one-off, static affair. To be truly useful in an ever-changing world, the RTVA must be a dynamic process that continually assesses as many factors as is feasible.

Objective 2: Conceive and implement the program according to best-practice family security standards

Continuous operational excellence is a key objective of any family protection program, and it is the responsibility of the family security manager to ensure that the team performs accordingly.

To do this, the security manager must establish standard operating procedures according to industry best practices for all team activities, as well as all metrics and key performance indicators to ensure that these are kept. These procedures must cover all aspects of protection, from advance work to after action reviews.

Of course, all of this must take place within the boundaries of available budgets. If budgetary constraints impinge on the manager's ability to deliver best-in-class protection, then the manager will have to lobby for more resources – and at the same time find creative ways to work within the budget.

Objective 3: Align the program with family culture and personal preferences

Because protection procedures sometimes fit like a square peg into the round hole of family routines, it is especially important that the family protection manager align the program with the family's way of doing things.

In order to deliver against this objective, the family protection manager must have good answers to many questions. How are the family's lifestyle goals best expressed in terms of family protection? What are the rules and policies – written and unwritten – that affect the program? Which values, norms, and shared assumptions make it easy to provide family protection – and which make it difficult? How do protective agents and managers best navigate through principal and family relationships?

We tell new agents working in a family protection team that one objective is "don't make the family think". By this, we mean that family protection agents need to fit naturally within the family's way of doing things, a.k.a. its culture. For example, saying "Good morning, Sir" might create a cumbersome moment that makes the principals think "Who is this guy?", instead of simply going about their lives. We're there to facilitate the family's lifestyle, not get in the way.

Unless personal preferences are included in the family protection program's objectives, the program is doomed to fail – simply because family members don't like it.

It all starts with a conversation. Security managers need to understand just what family members hope the security program will accomplish for them. Are they primarily concerned about something happening to them at home or in public? Or is it both? How important is it that security staff are in plain view or stay in the background? How would the family like to organize communication with the security team?

Security professionals should not expect family members to clearly articulate program goals. Rather, through conversations with either the family or their estate or family office staff, they should initiate an ongoing dialogue that enables the family and/or its representatives to describe what program success would look like to them. Once security managers understand the personal preferences of the principal and those of his or her family, they then must translate these into goals that the team can work toward. Making these explicit and measurable, i.e., turning them into key performance indicators (KPIs), is no easy task, but it is an essential one.

It is the family's vision of program success, transformed into transparent KPIs, that enables meaningful discussions at quarterly performance reviews. By holding actual team performance up to the family's agreed ideals on a regular basis, protection teams are able to correct performance gaps and consistently reinforce progress towards the ideal.

Chapter 9:
Training and background requirements for protective security positions

No matter what the candidate's background, specialized training is a prerequisite for work in protective security for families and individuals. The skills learned here complement those developed in law enforcement, the military, or other security-related fields, but are also different.

Training takes place in private schools. The good schools are run by professionals who have up-to-date, real-life protection experience and are also great teachers; and then there are all the other schools....

Below is what we look for in a protective security agent's training history:

Basic executive protection or residential security training: These introductory courses are offered by a number of private schools and vary in length and quality. Residential security jobs are often entry-level positions in the industry and dedicated training is a plus.

Emergency medical training: Executive protection professionals must be trained in cardiopulmonary resuscitation (CPR) and automated external defibrillator (AED) use and have first aid training at the healthcare-provider level to operate in our industry.

Evasive/antiterrorism driving: The ability to safely operate a motor vehicle is of paramount importance in family protection, and "security drivers" and "executive protection drivers" provide some of the most valuable functions on any team. It's often the first position on a team.

Defensive tactics: Training in some kind of martial art or other close-quarter defensive tactic is a definite plus. The particular method, or mix of methods, is not as important as a "cover and evacuate" mindset rather than a "stay and fight" mindset.

Foreign language skills: The ability to get by in other cultures is vital to international family security, and speaking more than one language is always a plus.

Protective advance work: Unfortunately, most security protection schools do not spend enough time on protective advance work, so we ask candidates how they have otherwise acquired and developed these skills.

Firearms: Armed protection details have been the exception rather than the rule, especially outside the United States. There are some indications that this is changing, however, and that demand for armed security is on the rise. In cases where executive protection details are armed, it is important to note that the use of firearms is very different from other armed security, law enforcement or military roles. Those who do participate in armed executive protection details require a radically different kind of training than that required in other armed roles.

Additional recommended courses:

- Transitional training for law enforcement, military and high-threat protection specialists
- Covert executive protection
- Use of force training
- Surveillance detection
- Etiquette training
- Event management training

Many kinds of experience can lead to a career in family security protection.

People with many different kinds of backgrounds make excellent careers in family security protection. Indeed, in our experience, success in family security protection depends primarily on the individual, not on his or her former career. We've seen rookies become professionals quickly, and we've seen seasoned professionals do a horrible job. Below are some of the most common backgrounds for corporate executive protection that can be applied to family protection:

Security: Typically, people with experience in security positions such as uniformed, plainclothes, residential, commercial, government or nonprofit. People with these backgrounds usually start in residential security but can easily go on to become great success stories and enjoy excellent careers in executive protection.

Law enforcement: The law enforcement officers (LEOs) we see come from federal, state or local agencies. The family security industry gets some immediate gratification from people with this background:

- Ability to drive extremely well

- Local knowledge

- Ability to deal with difficult people and de-escalate conflicts through verbal means

- Defensive tactics

- Natural ability to protect

Law enforcements officers who have not served in a dignitary or elected official protective detail must usually start out in entry-level positions. Because of the skills mentioned above, however, they usually do not stay at the entry level for very long.

Military: Since the military community is vast and diverse, we see applicants from every branch and virtually every function. The veterans who seem to do really well don't necessarily come from one specific branch or group. The most successful veterans are those who took the skills they learned in the military, then sought out the best private sector training they could find. Ultimately, it always comes down to the person and his or her ability to adapt. To adapt to family security, good transitional training and an openness to accepting an entry-level position are extremely helpful.

High-threat protection: This includes anyone working in a high-threat protective (HTP) capacity on behalf of a private security agency. Most of these folks have impressive military or law enforcement backgrounds prior to their work in the HTP community. Typically, the ones who have the most staying power in family security are those who had good transitional training.

Dignitary/diplomatic protection: While this term can cover several groups, we refer specifically to those who have worked in an official capacity for heads of state, royalty, departments of state, etc. As a rule of thumb, this group is suitable for mid-level family security positions but would also benefit from a high-quality executive protection course.

Celebrity/entertainment protection: Due to the heavy media exposure of their principals, and their occasional own on-camera roles interacting with paparazzi, these "bodyguards" are probably what most people think of when they consider close protection. Although there are many similarities, family security and celebrity protection are different animals. For example, it's common in Hollywood circles to take pictures with clients, and it may even be considered OK to geo-tag current client locations; these would be considered reasons for dismissal in family protection.

Corporate/high-net-worth executive protection: Of course, these are the jobs we most frequently hire for, and there are applicants who already have good experience in the field protecting C-level executives for Fortune 500 and other corporations, and/or experience protecting high-net-worth clients.

Chapter 10:
The key roles in family security programs

In this chapter, we take a closer look at the makeup of the team that will carry out the day-to-day protection of the principal and family.

All family security programs require a certain set of competencies and will include roughly the same types of job descriptions. They do so differently, however, according to program complexity and maturity. Most family security programs will require that the roles below be fulfilled at one level or another.

- Specialist partners
- Residential security agents
- Close protection agents
- Security driver
- Family protection manager
- Intelligence analyst

- Operations center agents

- Specialist partners as part of the protection team

We have included the role of specialist family protection partner on this must-have role list for a reason: Unless the plan is for operations on the scale of the U.S. president's Secret Service, it is simply not feasible to in-source all aspects of a modern family protection program.

This is most readily apparent with something like security drivers. While it might make good sense to hire a full-time security driver based at the principal's residence, for example, it would be neither efficient nor safe for a family program to bring drivers from the U.S. to India and Nepal for a short business trip. Local road conditions and traffic cultures are radically different, and a U.S. driver couldn't be expected to acquire the linguistic, cultural, navigational, and driving skills necessary to do the job properly for a three-day, two-country visit. What does make sense is using a specialist partner who can arrange for vetted security drivers, in many different places, who live up to the same high standards as those applied at home. A reliable specialist partner with global reach can be expected to coordinate such services and others.

Drawing on specialist partners is a reliable way to respond quickly to changing circumstances – which may well be the one constant of a busy family protection program. This is the fastest and most reliable way to add new roles to the overall protective team, whether it be a residential or close protection agent, an intelligence analyst, or practically anything else. If the principal's threat level suddenly increases, specialist partners can be drawn upon to fill the agent gap until more a permanent solution is found, or until the threat subsides. Similarly, specialist partners with well-established international networks can allow the program to scale flexibly, globally and quickly, without adding headcount.

Residential protection agents: Depending on the nature of the threats to the principal and his or her family, residential security will often be a foundational element of any family protection program.

Time and place predictability are two key factors that facilitate privacy invasions and physical attacks, and a person's home has plenty of both. Open-source searches can easily reveal where prominent people live; home is where most people spend as much time as they can.

While residential security is sometimes organized separately from the principal's executive protection, there are good reasons to integrate the two efforts into one program. For one thing, successful integration provides seamless coverage based on the same intelligence, managed by the same people, according to the same principles. For another, there can be some economies of scale in assigning interchangeable roles to some residential and close protection agents.

As described above, the skills and experience requirements for residential agents are lower than those for executive protection agents. This doesn't mean that residential agents are less important for overall program success, or that relationships between residential agents and the principal's family are less complex. In fact, relationships between residential agents and the principal can be MORE complex due to the extremely personal nature that can develop with these types of programs.

Maintaining trust while balancing discretion and protective professionalism requires a high degree of emotional intelligence. Finding people who display both the right soft and hard skills can have a huge impact here.

In our experience, working with residential agents can provide managers with a kind of recruitment pool for family protection positions: This gives managers a chance to see agents in action, then hand pick some of them for further training and other roles.

Security drivers: Security drivers are an important element of family protective programs. For one thing, they help mitigate one of the most pervasive risk factors of all, the banal traffic accident. For another, they significantly improve the productivity of the principal and other family members, who can concentrate on something besides driving during daily commutes and other local transportation.

Like residential agents, security drivers may or may not be integrated members of the permanent family protection team. Depending on program size and budgets, it sometimes makes good sense to let close protection agents double as security drivers and vice versa.

When the program requires frequent use of a trained driver in the same location, for example, to handle commutes between the principal's primary residence and workplace, then it often makes good organizational, protective, and economic sense to retain a dedicated person for this job. Conversely, as we pointed out above, it would make no sense to hire a driver in locations that the principal and his family visit only occasionally.

Close protection agents: A cornerstone of every advanced program, close protection agents, also known as executive protection agents, are responsible for providing close protection of the principals outside of the home. And as is the case for residential security agents, successful close protection agents also possess a unique mix of hard and soft skills and experience.

These are the persons who create and enforce the actual circle of protection around the principal and family as they move out of their residence and through their day – both at the office, school, and while travelling. They perform advance work when new locations need to be scouted and made safe. They are on the frontline of ongoing security and productivity optimization for the principal, making sure that logistics are as smooth as they can be and constantly adjusting plans and activities as needs be.

We are often asked how many family protection agents are necessary to staff a program. Of course, the answer depends on the scope and nature of the program. In our experience, however, at least two full-time agents are needed to create the backbone of a good program, and this can be considered the minimum viable number of dedicated agents. This does not mean that two agents can provide full 24/7/365 coverage for any given principal. It does mean that a minimal team of a family protection manager and two agents can provide excellent service (with the help of specialist partners as needed) and be a good foundation on which to build.

Such a two-person team is enough to provide solid coverage on a multi-country trip. The manager stays at home, and the two agents leapfrog between destinations. While the first agent is with the principal (and family) in one country, the second agent is in the next country doing advance work and double-checking necessary third-party resources such as security drivers, vehicles or additional protective agents sourced through a specialist partner. This second agent stays in country to welcome the principal (and family) and handles security while he or she is there; meanwhile, the first agent moves on the next stop on the itinerary to do advance work there.

Close protection agents can be either full-time employees or embedded from a specialist partner. Embedding agents from a partner has the advantage of allowing both the security manager and the principal to try out different agents to find those with the best fit with the principal's and family lifestyle and culture. This can be a significant plus: Despite all efforts to match the right people to the right jobs, the only way to really discover whether chemistry and personalities work well together in this people business is to try it out. If the family has to recruit, hire and fire to find the right people, this takes time and money that can be saved by drawing on a partner's deep bench.

The family protection manager: The family protection manager provides leadership, management and accountability. This is the person who translates strategy into operations; leads and organizes the protection team; and acts as the bridge between the protection team, the principal, and the family office ecosystem. The manager is the one point of contact that all stakeholders look to – and hold responsible for – all aspects of the program.

Depending on the scope of the program, the role of family protection manager can be filled in a variety of ways. But it should always be filled: It is essential that one person have overall responsibility for the program, and that this is clear to the estate manager, the principals, and other stakeholders.

Initially, a brand new family program might bring in a specialist partner on a consultant basis to act as part-time program manager and help set up the program. This has the advantage of using a skilled practitioner who can draw on experience from other family protection programs. Once the program is ready to be implemented, a solution that provides ongoing resources will be necessary.

Some family protection programs might take another approach in their early stages and go the route of retaining one person with the dual role of local security driver and family protection coordinator, but not manager. When this person is not driving, he or she is able to work on other aspects of the program, such as liaising with a specialist partner to hire security drivers in other locations.

Once the decision to create a more comprehensive family security protection program has been made, the best way to begin organizing it is to assign it a manager. It will then be the manager's responsibility to ensure that the program is based on an up-to-date Risk, Threat, and Vulnerability Analysis (RTVA), write a suitable strategy, plan and organize program implementation, staff up, and ultimately run the program. Of course, all of this must be done with respect for the family's culture and the principal's personal preferences, and in cooperation with the key stakeholders described in Chapter 4.

The manager can be either hired directly by the family, or "embedded" from a specialist partner. This second option has the advantage of placing the onus of recruiting and developing a new manager on an organization that has a proven track record and deep bench for doing just that – something few family security or family office HR departments have any experience in.

The ideal family protection manager will be a person with the right background and personality, who has come up through the ranks as a protection agent and understands all practical aspects of the profession, and who has experience in running programs in family settings.

A manager will often take a shift as a protection agent for a number of reasons. This could be to fill the occasional scheduling gap and should be to stay close to the front lines in order to evaluate program and agent performance. The manager needs to discover and correct any issues that can affect program goals, and coach agents accordingly.

At the same time, it is important that the roles of manager and agent not be conflated. If the manager falls into the trap of becoming the default, more-or-less permanent protection agent, then there will be no time to take care of managerial tasks. The manager who continues to act as an agent shirks the work of organizing, planning and maintaining relations across the family ecosystem. The tough decisions about hiring, developing, and perhaps firing protection agents do not receive the attention they should. Not only does the manager-cum-agent run the clear risk of jeopardizing program success, personal burnout is all but guaranteed.

Intelligence analyst: After residential and close protection agents, security drivers, and a security manager, the next full-time staff of a high-performing family security program should consider is that of intelligence analyst. Of course, this adds cost and complexity, and is not for new or streamlined programs. But when budgets and managerial prowess allow, its advantages are many.

One of the first and most concerning risks facing a prominent person and his or her family is the unwanted attention they receive from "People of Interest" (POIs) or "Groups of Interest" (GOIs). What threat do these POIs and GOIs actually pose? When and where should we be concerned about them? What can we do about them? What should we do about them? A solid protective intelligence analysis/threat management program can provide answers to these questions. Identifying, investigating, monitoring, and recommending appropriate responses to mitigate risk are all part of the core job responsibilities.

But intelligence analysts keep an eye on more than POIs and GOIs. Basing current protection on old intelligence can easily give a false impression that the team is shaping its protective efforts according to a true picture of the principal's actual prominence and its resultant risks, when in fact it is not. An outdated, stale RTVA can be worse than no RTVA.

The protective intelligence analyst is charged with ongoing updates of the RTVA, which is critical to stay on top of the changing risk and threat scenarios that impact the principal and his or her family. In addition to these updates, the intelligence analyst may also be tasked with preparing regular reports on other security-related issues important to the principal and family, or with writing ad hoc reports for destinations on the principal's itinerary.

The intelligence analyst may be hired directly by the corporation, the principal or the family office staff, or embedded. Embedding the analyst from a specialist partner lets him or her draw on the partner's entire worldwide network as well as on the principal's own resources.

Chapter 11:
How to determine appropriate staffing levels for family protective security programs

Some of the most common questions we get from new clients concern staffing levels. What are our options? What have families with similar needs done before us? How many people do we need to set up a program, and what kinds of people do they need to be?

This is a natural line of questioning. Those tasked with starting up new family security programs often have little or no experience in the field or track record for reference. This can also be the case for those with protective backgrounds from the government: Cultural norms vary widely between the public and private sectors, as do budgetary considerations and organizational expectations.

For the family in need of security, this is also a crucial line of questioning. The success of security programs depends directly on the quality and quantity of their staff. Providers must be able to clearly explain what kinds of people and how many of them are needed, what their responsibilities will be, how much they will cost, and what value they add to the family's security. Programs that are understaffed lead to burnout, invite favoritism, and generally perform poorly, defeating our purpose of keeping the principal and his or her family safe, happy, and productive. Ultimately, such programs fail to demonstrate their value and will either be replaced or terminated – often along with those responsible for making the staffing decisions.

In addition to their performance and operational issues, under-dimensioned protection programs usually suffer a slow death for other reasons. When those tasked with managing and organizing the program get stuck in the tactical weeds of doing endless shifts, they neglect their strategic leadership roles. They simply don't have, and should not be expected to have, the skills to be both the on-the-ground protective agents and to establish and maintain the necessary relationships throughout the family office and estate ecosystems. Thus, there is no one to create and maintain transparency between the program and other stakeholders or work for a shared understanding of program value – the consequences of which can be as debilitating for sustainable program viability as poor operational performance.

There are two sets of attributes that leaders of successful family protection programs need to master. The first of these concerns the program leader's personality traits regarding:

Persuasion and influence: Does the leader find a way to make things happen working with and through others – and at the same time treat them with respect and dignity?

Focus on the big picture and attention to detail: Is the leader able to keep an eye on overarching goals while paying meticulous attention to the minutiae that cumulatively make a difference?

Strategic planning: Has the leader demonstrated success in implementing systems and processes in a methodical way to reach a goal, and develop programs over time?

The second set of attributes has to do with the leader's ability to run a business. Family security programs are a paid service, and whether their leaders have transferable business skills from other contexts or not, they must see themselves as responsible for their "business'" sustained success. Thus, leaders must have demonstrable skills in operations and more.

Operations: This is where the rubber hits the road, where management of people performing the proper tactical procedures, consistently and efficiently, deliver agreed results. Without solid operations, there is no security.

Finance and administration: Just as in any other business, no one likes financial surprises or sloppy bookkeeping. Good family security managers need to understand the numbers and keep track of them.

People development: Real leaders understand that their success depends completely on the success of their people. That's why they get good at attracting the right talent, then retaining and developing the people who perform well.

Business development: Whether they are directly hired or working via an outsourced specialist partner, good leaders take care of their security programs with the zeal of a start-up founder. They recognize and seize new opportunities. They stay true to their vision but are ready to pivot when circumstances demand it. And they are tireless communicators who always maintain good stakeholder relations by consistently listening to their clients' needs and demonstrate the program's value-add by making sure everyone understands its features and benefits.

Plenty of people are strong in one or several attributes but fall short of comprehensive mastery. Family security programs that enjoy long-term success are led by people who demonstrate ability in all of the above, both personality traits and business skills.

So how do you staff a family protective security program?

As we have pointed out many times before, there are no cookie-cutter protection solutions. Staffing levels for family security programs depend on program goals, which in turn must be needs-based. And the only real way to determine a principal's and his or her family's risk mitigation needs is to perform a Risk, Threat, and Vulnerability Analysis (RTVA) that takes into account the principal's prominence, known threats, work and travel routines, personal preferences, and a host of the family's factors. Once this improved situational awareness has been established, staffing can then be considered.

What are the staffing variables?

Those responsible for introducing family security services to the principal and his or her family must present staffing needs in a way that is understandable to others who most often have no experience in the field. To do this, it's helpful to break things down along the lines of the most important variables that must be considered.

The single most important staffing variable is ***coverage:*** When and in which situations does the principal and his or her family require protection, and how much protection is necessary? Should the program include residential protection only? Or do circumstances also dictate that security drivers for local commuting/travel be included? What about personal protection when the principal or family members are at work, school, going about their lives at home, and traveling?

As we will see in the explanatory scenarios below, coverage needs vary from residential only to much more. It's important to remember here both the principal's and his or her family's personal lifestyle, preferences and culture – and what a principal and his or her family may want in terms of coverage (for example, as little and as unobtrusive as possible) may not be what a board-mandated program would prescribe (as comprehensive as possible).

In addition to coverage, or time spent *protecting* the principal and his or her family, we also need to consider **training, physical fitness and other professional development requirements:** time spent *preparing* to take care of the principal and his or her family. Some protection skills are rarely used but critical to have; others are perishable and need to be refreshed on a regular basis. Training needs must be addressed openly as part of staffing level discussions.

The other key staffing variable is the **types of personnel** needed. The most common choices here are the protective program manager and residential security agents, but other roles such as security drivers, executive protection agents, intelligence analysts, and more may also be relevant in more comprehensive programs.

The **make/buy decision** must also be considered. Although a needs-based staff headcount should, everything else being equal, remain the same whether or not all or parts of the program are outsourced, organizational relationships do make a difference. For example, hiring a specialist partner with enough skills and knowledge can allow the principal and the family to benefit from scale advantages more flexibly without ramping up headcount.

Finally, we also need to understand **the availability of other security resources** upon which the family security protection program can draw. If the principal's company already has its own executive protection, intelligence analysts, or global security operations center (GSOC), for example, this may impact the scoping of the family security protection program and headcount.

Scenario 1: Staffing a full-time residential protection program

Let's start by getting a handle on staffing levels for a residential security program consisting of two team members to provide protection for one estate 24/7/365. Two-member teams are able to handle many standard security procedures and are absolutely necessary so that one team member can take a break while the other doesn't. We consider this to be the minimum coverage for a well-functioning residential security program.

First, let's think about how many team members are necessary. Although some teams use eight-hour shifts, the most common way to organize residential shifts is in twelve-hour chunks, which reduces hand-off issues for teams and creates more continuity with fewer shift changes for the principals. This gives two shifts per day or four shifts per day for a two-member team. Then let's divide the total number of coverage hours needed per week by 40, the average workweek, to get a rough idea of how many full-time equivalent (FTE/s) employees we're going to need: 7 x 24 = 168; 168 x 2 = 336; 336 / 40 = 8.4 FTEs. Finally, we need to consider absences due to vacations, training, and illnesses, as well as the consequences of scheduling nights and weekends. Depending on jurisdictions, labor laws, and contracts, all of this will mean that the 8.4 FTEs needed to cover all shifts actually grows to 10-12 FTEs as a minimum.

These 10-12 team members can do a lot, but they cannot manage themselves. A program like this also requires a manager to provide leadership. Appointing one of the team members working regular security shifts as a manager is guaranteed to turn out badly. The program manager must be able to use all of his or her time to develop the program and its people, organize the staff and scheduling, work with other estate stakeholders, and handle a myriad of other issues as they arise.

Scenario 2: Staffing a full-time residential security protection program – and adding EP and security driving for the primary principal

Residential security will be enough for some principals, but most also require close protection at least in some circumstances. If the principal needs security drivers and executive protection, what kind of staffing levels should we expect?

To answer this question, we need to make some assumptions. First, let's assume that the principal has a workweek similar to many of our clients, i.e., an average of 60 hours per week, with spikes up to 80 hours and slow weeks down to 40.

Then, let's remember that security drivers and protection agents work even longer hours than the principal. They must arrive at the pickup point well before the designated time and they leave the final drop-off point only after the principal has been securely installed there, and all reporting and prep tasks have been wrapped up. This adds an average of two working hours per day to that of the principal. That gives us a weekly total of 10 hours in addition to the principal's 60, or an average of 70 agent hours per week. That's 1.75 full-time agents before we even start talking about training, professional development, time off due to vacations, illness, etc. So, let's call this two full-time staff for protecting the principal while working but not traveling.

Let's also assume that the principal travels a week or two out of most months, as most do, both domestically and internationally, often with multiple destinations on each trip. Depending on risk profiles and itineraries, this will require at least one additional agent, and typically two if one will be performing advance work while the other is providing close protection and traveling with the principal.

While the traveling duo is on the road, the at-home duo has time to engage in required training and for personal time off. And vice versa.

And let's not forget that this program also needs a manager – both to organize, develop, provide guidance to, and follow up on the four agents, but also to interface with other stakeholders, including the residential team and key members of the family office and estate. Again, placing someone in the double role of manager and working agent is not a sustainable option. We've never seen it work for long, but we have seen it create a lot of problems.

This brings us to a total of four to five full-time staff – one manager and four agents – as a minimally viable, full-time staff that provides protection during the principal's working hours. In addition to these close protection team members, we should factor in two security drivers, bringing the total number of staff needed in this scenario to approximately 20.

It should be remembered that even with a team of this size, it is still probable that the family would need to engage a reliable specialist partner to fill in the gaps and be ready for any unexpected rise in demand for services

Scenario 3: Staffing a comprehensive, complex and multifaceted security protection program for an entire family

Our final scenario includes everything mentioned above and more.

Such complex scenarios might provide protection for spouses and children, multiple residences, non-work travel and leisure activities, yachts, planes, etc. They might also comprise additional security services including event risk mitigation, intelligence analysis programs, covert protection and surveillance detection, and GSOC support.

We won't go through all the possible variants of such advanced programs – there are simply too many. Suffice it to say that staffing levels and managerial responsibilities increase with additional protectees and services.

Why families use a trusted specialist partner to help dimension programs

In our experience, few families have the experience or insight necessary to build their own family security protection programs – much less to accurately determine staffing needs and actually run them. Although it might look simple, just as professional golfers make the game look easy, it's a niche expertise.

Whether the principal and family eventually start and staff their own program or outsource some or all services, we recommend that they work with a trusted specialist partner when scoping program design and staffing. They are much more likely to arrive at sustainable organizational structures – and far less likely to build in the kinds of preventable program risks involved with starting a new protection program or fixing one that has run into trouble.

No program success without sufficient headcount

One of the easiest organizational traps to fall into, especially for new or growing programs, is insufficient staffing. To ensure success, it is critical that programs be staffed realistically.

Once the manager has found and developed a handful of good residential and close protection agents, it can be tempting to rely on the same small cadre – even though this can turn into 80-hour workweeks for the people involved. And although agents who thrive are resilient, resourceful, and self-motivated, as we saw in Chapter 10, even super agents can become overworked. This reduces their cognitive, physical, and operational readiness, of course, but it harms the program in other ways, too. Under-staffing is a short-sighted way to build a security program. It makes people lose attention to detail. It promotes complacency and fosters low morale. In time, excessive overtime erodes the hard and soft skills of any agent. In the longer term, of course, this kind of work-life balance is intolerable. Even the best and most dedicated of agents will find someplace else to work.

Favoritism is not the friend of successful protection programs

In the short and middle terms, relying heavily on just a few people increases the likelihood of favoritism between the principal, manager, and agents. While it's common and happens far too easily, favoritism is a bad thing. Period. Protection is a team sport, and in addition to promoting burnout, favoritism seriously reduces overall team effectiveness. It almost never ends well for the favorite one or anyone else.

It's one thing to make sure the program respects the principal's personal preferences – also regarding the kind of agent that provides protection. But it's another thing altogether to think that only a few individuals can fill this role. Unless the entire team develops sufficient understanding and responsiveness to the principal's preferences, it is doomed to fail.

In order to prevent favoritism, it is critical that ALL team members are clearly expected to know and understand the principal's specific preferences and perform accordingly. All relevant procedures must be documented with respect to these preferences and the program manager must ensure that they are being followed consistently. Importantly, the manager MUST have the conversation about the dangers and risks of favoritism with team members, the principals, and other relevant stakeholders throughout the estate ecosystem. Combatting favoritism, the insidious virus that sneaks up on a team and can kill it, should also be part of any quarterly review to keep it front and center for everyone.

Chapter 12:
Motivating and communicating with the family security team

Everybody knows that communication is the lifeblood of the organization and one of the manager's most essential tasks. In fact, managers typically spend far more time communicating than on other managerial tasks such as setting objectives, organizing, following up, and developing people.

If you think about it, the reasons for this are obvious. Without communicating program objectives clearly and consistently, the team won't know about them. Plans are meaningless when they stay in the manager's head. Key performance indicators (KPIs) and corrective action instructions are worthless unless they are told, discussed, and finally understood and internalized.

And yet survey after survey reveals that the most common employee complaint about management, across many types of organizations, is poor communication.

Although we have no statistics on the state of communication in the executive protection or family security industries, we're quite sure they would reveal a similar tendency. On the list of what makes or breaks good family protection programs, effective communication will always be at the top.

Especially important due to what we do

Given the criticality of what we do, protecting the wellbeing and productivity of the individual principal and his or her loved ones, the importance of good communication is only greater.

When communication breaks down – within the team, between the team and the principal, or between the team and other key stakeholders in the family ecosystem – program failure is just around the corner.

And when family protection programs fail, the principal's security and productivity are the first victims. The security manager's job security could be the next.

Overcoming communication challenges in family security

Family security managers face a number of particular communication challenges. It is important that they – as well as everyone else involved including team members, principals, family members, estate employees, family office, and other stakeholders – be aware of them.

One set of challenges arises because the stakeholders with whom we communicate are many and varied. On any one day, the manager may be selecting agents to protect the principal's preschool daughter, writing a budget report or giving feedback on a security driver in Nepal. Regardless, positive outcomes of these examples depend heavily on good communication by the family security manager.

But the biggest challenge is probably due to the fact that individual characteristics play such an important role in our field. Compared to other endeavors, the nature of our work puts a lot of focus on team members' personalities and people skills. Whereas a prickly bookkeeper might go far in corporate finance, or an eccentric marketer could enjoy a solid career as long as her campaigns create results, family security agents whose temperaments strike the principal as odd will not be long in that position – just like housekeepers, tutors, or nannies. Communicating directly and often about issues that are closely related to a colleague's psychological makeup is by no means easy; but it is always important in family security management.

The hallmarks of good communication for family security managers

Because of the special nature of what we do, family security managers need to take a special approach to communication. We outline below some key characteristics of good communication in family security programs that need constant managerial focus – and the understanding of all stakeholders.

360-degree: As we pointed out in Chapter 4, family security managers need to ensure good relationships throughout the family ecosystem. This includes the principal and his or her family members, of course, but also everyone on estate staffs, and some in family offices. It also includes everyone on the protection team, no matter where or when they work.

Family security managers need to make 360-degree communication a priority. This means regular meetings, phone calls, and reports; it also means making the most of each and every touch point that presents itself, whether it's a quick conversation between details or popping into someone's office when the opportunity arises.

Of course, some stakeholders are more important than others and should be prioritized. But it must also be a priority to make the rounds.

Proactive: Family security managers cannot afford the luxury of waiting to see what happens and then coming up with a plan. They need to think ahead, look around the corner, and be prepared for a range of eventualities before they materialize.

It helps the family security manager to think proactively in all things communicative, too. Through regular dialogue with the estate manager, for example, the security manager is always keen to discover issues while they are still small and fixable. What happened this week? What's happening next week? Why? How are we doing, and is there anything that we can do better?

Immediately responsive: When a family security manager discovers something that needs attention, it's important to respond quickly.

This illustrates the criticality of what we do: When the well-being of the principal we are assigned to protect is concerned, postponing communication to a more convenient or comfortable time is not an option. We need to act on available information now, not save it for a yearly performance review.

Responsiveness is also necessitated by the personal nature of what we do. If the principal signals dissatisfaction with a team member, for example, it's better to act now rather than later: A quick coaching session might nip the problem in the bud. And if a personnel issue has already grown beyond repair, it's up to the manager to take decisive action, and quickly communicate this, even though the message is not a pleasant one.

Direct: There can be no beating around the bush when it comes to management communication in family security programs. Goals and expectations need to be crystal clear to all involved. Changing standard operating procedures (SOPs) must be expressed with absolute precision and without ambiguity. The same holds true for explaining and clarifying the needs of the principal and the family to staff members.

Being brutally honest does not have to mean being brutal, however. While direct communication that protects program integrity always takes precedence above other matters, it does matter that the manager treats everyone with civility. It is possible to be both completely honest and direct in one's communication, and to do so with respect and empathy. In fact, it is absolutely necessary to achieve a well-run protection program.

Continual: Managers who are good communicators never rest on their laurels and take a break from communicating. They treat communication as a constant priority. They include regular meetings or calls in their plans; and they always find ways to leverage any touch point to establish a stakeholder dialogue.

Managers are ambassadors for the team's brand and reputation. They take opportunities to educate, provide metrics that demonstrate performance, and tell stories of how the team added value in different scenarios. Transparency and understanding are the goal; targeted, thoughtful communication is the way to achieve it.

Across time and geographic barriers: Communicating with the entire family protection team means being available when and where people work. If some team members work only the graveyard shift of a residential detail, then the manager needs to make the time – and the effort – to show up and talk to people, even though it's late.

Everyone on the team needs to be acknowledged and to know that he or she is an important part of the whole. They must know that they are connected to the mothership even though they might not see it every day, and that the manager is aware of and interested in individual performance and ready to provide support as needed.

If team members do not feel this close connection, then there is a real risk that they will not be up-to-date on changes in SOPs or principal's requirements. The probability of them becoming complacent increases; and the likelihood of the manager discovering the resultant drop in team readiness decreases.

Chapter 13:
Measuring the performance of the family protective team: The importance of KPIs

Even if you don't have much experience in family security, it's easy for anyone with any kind of management background to imagine many questions that you would want answers to:

- Are the customers (the principal and family) happy with the service? Has anyone asked them or has this just been assumed?

- Are there onsite training and standard operating procedure (SOP) manuals for staff? How are they used on a regular basis? When were they last updated?

- Have all employees completed the required training? When was the last training conducted and was it relevant to program goals?

- Are issues and challenges communicated smoothly between the security manager, the principals, and other stakeholders?

- Are the agents happy in their work? Is this shown in the way they perform, speak, and carry themselves?

- Do staff receive quarterly or yearly evaluations? Do they know the standards they are graded on?

- Is there a persons of interest (POI) list? How does the protection team stay up-to-date on these POIs, and how do they report incidents with them?

- Does the team know how to use the gear required for their job? Is the gear in good working order?

The best way to ensure satisfactory answers to these and more questions is to transform them into key performance indicators (KPIs) and make performance management an integrated part of family security.

Questions are good. Specific KPIs and effective follow up are even better

As any successful manager knows, what gets measured gets done. Family security protection is no different.

Developing a strong set of key performance indicators – and then relentlessly following up on them – is essential to program success. A disciplined approach to KPIs helps the family protection manager and other stakeholders in several ways:

Focus: Good KPIs keep the family protection team focused on what matters. The emphasis should be on goals that are shared and important – i.e., the ones that define the contours of program success as agreed with the family and other stakeholders.

Diagnostics: KPIs help management get a clear picture of what's working well and what needs improvement. For family security, where people are the program's most important asset, KPIs need to track both qualitative as well as quantitative aspects of team performance.

Accountability: When it comes to security teams, personal accountability is key. There must be no doubt about who is responsible for what. Solid, personalized KPIs enable team members to see how they contribute – and managers to understand who is/is not performing to reach program goals.

Preemptive corrective action: Ongoing evaluations allow family protection managers to identify norms and outliers over time, so they can proactively respond to performance developments before trouble hits.

Transparency: Even in successful family security programs, it is not uncommon to be asked "What do you guys actually do, anyway?" The KPI reporting helps demonstrate that family protection is more like a fire department than a police department. When we're not fighting fires, we're getting better at it by practicing.

Key performance indicators are not the same as metrics. Metrics measure individual data points, whereas KPIs are sets of quantifiable metrics that enable the family protection manager as well as principals and other stakeholders to evaluate performance against strategic and operational goals.

Reviewing key program metrics on a regular basis, e.g., at 30- and 90-day intervals, both internally and with the client, is critical to program success. By analyzing metrics and KPI results, these reviews should make clear exactly what teams do and how what they do adds value. They should also highlight the achievements and challenges of the last review period and set goals for the next.

Essentially, these reviews provide answers to – and preempt – the question no security manager wants to hear: "What do you guys actually do, anyway?" Maintaining full operational transparency so no one has to ask that question is a good way to keep programs on track.

Best-practice KPIs for family security

While the KPIs for individual family security programs will vary according to circumstances, best practice dictates that they all share the same basic characteristics.

Aligned with program goals: KPIs should always help us understand program performance compared to program goals. While any individual KPI – or its underlying metrics – will not necessarily explain program success or failure, a good KPI report will let us understand whether the family protection program is meeting its stated objectives – and to what extent.

Important: You don't need to measure everything, just the important things. But sometimes important KPIs are made up of multiple metrics, none of which seems too significant in and of themselves. For example, knowing how many hours team members spend on travel might not appear that critical, but the data can enable decisions on hiring remote staff and reduce overall program costs – as well as readiness. Similarly, because it is vital to monitor risk factors that can affect the principal's and family's safety, correlations that affect prominence – for example, increased media exposure through planned PR activities – may be meaningful, as are travel days in emerging markets.

Understandable: It might seem obvious, but we've seen so many examples to the contrary that we want to point out that KPIs must be understandable for all involved. Security professionals have a tendency to rely on jargon and acronyms that family stakeholders might find difficult to comprehend. Be sure to translate tactical speak into transparent KPIs.

Measurable: The KPIs must, of course, be based on measurable data. In a people business like ours, however, we should not shy away from personal evaluations that hard-nosed accountants might sneer at. KPIs for family security can be qualitative as well as quantitative.

Consistent: Over time, KPI reports let us understand developments and trends that might otherwise be difficult to spot. To be sure that we are comparing apples to apples, the underlying data should be collected and correlated in a consistent way.

Timely: Some things need to get evaluated sooner rather than later in order to provide value. For example, a KPI review after every detail lets us learn lessons that can be applied immediately.

Don't forget to keep track of team morale and cultural fit

Family protection is a team effort, so evaluating the family security team's cohesiveness and ability to work together is important. Here are some things to consider for ongoing evaluation:

Shared sense of purpose: The family protection team and key stakeholders must clearly understand the risks and threats to principals and family – and the benefits of mitigating those risks in a way that enhances productivity. The family protection team is seen as a valuable partner in supporting the safety, satisfaction, and productivity of identified principals and their families.

Shared sense of team standards and approach: It is essential that the team understand and use transparent operational standards for everything from simple scheduling to crisis procedures.

Good relationships and communication: Frictionless interactions within the team and between the team and key stakeholders is essential to program success. Though not as simple to capture as other metrics, KPIs should nonetheless be developed in order to evaluate how family protection team members cooperate with each other and relevant personnel.

Good program fit with the principal's and family's personal preferences and culture: When family protection teams achieve excellence, their presence is effective but unobtrusive. They facilitate productivity and security without being asked to do so, and often without being noticed; they never make the principal think twice or miss a beat, but rather adjust to the family culture and the principal's lifestyle.

Excellent team moral and readiness: It is common – and potentially disastrous – for family protection teams to grow complacent. Nothing happening to the principal can easily be confused with program success. That is why it is essential to develop KPIs that track team members' morale and operational readiness.

Potential KPI areas for family security protection

There is no one-size-fits-all KPI list for family security protection. Your ideal set will depend on whether your program is in startup, turnaround or sustain mode, and on specific program objectives. Nonetheless, see below for a number of factors that will be relevant for many programs and around which KPIs may be developed.

- Ongoing risk assessment
  - Principal and family prominence
  - Travel destination risks
  - Intel including social media monitoring
  - Persons of interest
- Key stakeholder satisfaction
  - Principal/family feedback
  - Principal productivity
- Key partner feedback
  - Program/vendor management
  - Estate management and other estate staff
  - Family office stakeholders
  - Executive administrators
  - Corporate security or executive protection teams
  - Specialist partner vendors
- Responsiveness
  - Availability and appropriateness of family security resources
  - Issues addressed thoroughly and quickly
  - Short notice request performance

- Quality of services provided
  - Program management/organization
  - Deliverables
  - On ground support (agents and transportation)
  - Administrative activities
- Team workload
  - Travel days
  - Domestic trips
  - International trips
  - Comp time
- Readiness
  - Training
  - Drills
  - Fitness evaluation
- Quality of communications
  - Appropriate
  - Accurate
  - Clear and concise
- Operational transparency
  - Execution to expectations
  - Clear understanding of family security protection program by key stakeholders
- Financial performance
  - Budget expectations set and met – good financial stewardship
  - Responsiveness to identified issues

Chapter 14:
Recruiting and developing the people on the family protective security team

Residential security, security driving, and close protection are niche skills. As we saw above in Part I, to be successful at them requires a certain amount of talent, specific training, and experience. As we'll see below in Part IV, being born with the right kind of personality doesn't hurt, either.

Recruiting suitable residential security agents, security drivers, close protection agents, and family security managers is a niche skill, too. It requires a fair amount of dedicated human resources experience within this relatively narrow vertical market to effectively attract, evaluate, and select candidates who will ultimately create value for family security programs – and achieve success in their next job and entire career.

To give those with no experience in hiring family security personnel an idea of some of the necessary recruitment processes, we mention here just a few of the elements our own HR department considers to be essential when recruiting candidates for family protection jobs.

A strong employer brand: Organizations that have good reputations in the industry are more likely to attract the best candidates.

Competitive wages and benefits: Although money is not everything, money does matter. We consider this to be a necessary but not sufficient condition for hiring the best candidates.

The possibility to grow and learn in the job: For some, a good job in residential security is all a person can ask for. Such employees can be great at their work, and enjoy long careers doing so. For others, a good job in residential security is only the beginning; they consider such work to be entry-level and are eager to move on to bigger and better things. Organizations that offer career paths and the ability to try out different positions in different places are more likely to attract the brightest bulbs.

Effective search and selection processes: As in other fields, broad and deep networking throughout the industry always helps, as does the ability to filter and prioritize potential candidates efficiently. In our industry, this might include:

- Initial completion of non-disclosure agreements and background check authorization forms

- Submission and review of relevant professional licenses and credentials

- Background checks as relevant and as applicable due to local legislation concerning criminal record, driving

record, sex offender record, drug screening, prior employers, personal references, etc.

- Psychological and physical fitness testing as relevant

- A series of one-on-one interviews with our own HR
experts and with client stakeholders

Background: Where do we find the best candidates for protective security positions

Appropriate personnel for a program can have many different backgrounds. They might come from specialty security
agencies, such as the Secret Service, or be former law enforcement officers. They could have experience in the military or in
an intelligence agency. They might have a B.A. in psychology or
no degree at all.

As we will see below in Part IV, however, regardless of their
previous experience, successful agents and managers need to
demonstrate a number of personality traits. In order to get
things done and meet the principal's goals, these security personnel may need to collaborate with nannies, philanthropic
program managers, public relations teams, celebrities, chiefs of
staff for presidents and prime ministers, and cleaning staff – all
on the same day.

They must be able to blend into family environments and
have the agility to customize their support on the fly, balancing
the principal's preferences with best-practice risk mitigation
whatever the circumstances.

In our experience, family estates and family offices rarely
have the experience to be successful, on their own, in this niche
HR domain. Hiring a specialist partner for parts or all of the
recruitment process can prevent many of the most common HR

pitfalls; it can also allow a family to "test drive" prospective personnel (as full-time contracted resources) for a period of 6 to 12 months before committing.

Developing people is the best way to ensure sustainable performance

It's been true for generations, and it's especially resonant with Generation Y, the so-called Millennials born between the early 80s and 00s, who are now pursuing their careers. Money motivates, of course, but the opportunity to learn and grow professionally is what really turns a wage earner into a passionate and dedicated team member.

People who are not developing in their jobs feel like they're treading water instead of making career progress. The good ones will move on to find somewhere where they can learn more and take on more responsibility. The less talented will stay on – and these are not the people we want to depend on to keep our principals safe, happy, and productive.

What does this mean for family security managers? Plenty. If managers don't develop talent, they lose it. If those responsible for family protection don't help their staff develop and learn, then they don't deserve to be called managers. For, in addition to all of the other responsibilities that fall upon them, spotting and nurturing talent is an absolutely essential cornerstone of a sustainable family security program.

When managers own this responsibility and dedicate serious effort to it, good things happen. The best talent will naturally gravitate to their programs. Team motivation and performance will be reliably high. Staff turnover will be predictably low.

But when managers prove unwilling to or incapable of developing people, the opposite will occur. Talent will seep away, often citing "I got a better offer somewhere else" as the reason. Of course, these people are smart enough not to burn their bridges to a former employer, so they would never tell the truth at their exit interviews: They're moving on because their manager failed to take their developmental needs seriously and didn't help them learn new skills or grow into new responsibilities.

Keeping perishable skills fresh through training

As we saw in Chapter 9, there are a number of skills that protection personnel need to possess because they are vitally important to our overall goal: mitigating risk to the principal and family to an acceptable level. These include basic and advanced family security protection skills, security driving, and first aid.

Fortunately, of course, agents rarely, if ever, need to call on skills such as operating a heart defibrillator or engaging in evasive driving. This doesn't mean these skills are unimportant or irrelevant, however. Family security managers need to realize that these are all perishable skills. If agents don't use them, they lose them.

That is why regular training schedules need to be developed for all teams and all agents. Some of this training will be off site at dedicated facilities and with specialized instructors. Some of it will take place around a conference table at team meetings and be conducted by the manager or a team member with subject matter expertise. All of it is important.

More than once, we've run into family offices who roll their eyes at our requirements to keep something as essential as security driving skills up-to-date. Didn't the agent just do that 18 months ago? Isn't zipping around a racetrack at high speed more fun than necessary? When has anything ever happened while the principal or his or her family was being driven around town?

These are all reasonable questions for people with no experience in family security. In these cases and many others, the manager needs to step up and explain the importance of ongoing training both to develop and retain the best talent and to meet the program's goals of protecting the principal and family.

The importance of clear career paths

Career development planning has been a staple of corporate HR for decades. Now, some people are finally waking up to the fact that family security programs also rely on professionals who pursue career opportunities – if not here, then somewhere else where they are more readily available.

As our industry develops and more and more corporations and high net worth families begin to implement protective programs, the importance of clearly defined career development plans continues to grow – albeit from a woefully low base. Far too many agents stay in the same jobs for far too long without developing new skills or increasing their level of responsibility. If we do not improve, we will soon see bottlenecks as more companies and families require good protection managers but find it difficult to fill the positions.

The bad news is that it's necessary even to raise this issue. As an industry, we have been far too haphazard in how we develop people as part of professionalizing our services. Corporations and families have relied on retired law enforcement officers or military veterans whose careers were more in sunset than start-up mode. Along with them, specialist partner providers within corporate and family security have not done enough to improve career planning and development. This has to change.

The good news is that we don't need to reinvent the wheel to bring on significant improvements. We can start by borrowing tried-and-true methods honed by corporate HR departments the world over, such as systems for spotting and nurturing high performance employees, formalized career development plans for everyone, improved coaching and mentoring skills for managers, and aligning job classifications, salaries, and benefits against clearly defined career milestones.

Informal versus formal learning...

Now, it might be tempting simply to bring in some HR consultants to set up a formalized system of training and career development for family security programs, throw some money at them, then sit back to wait for results. Sorry, but while this might all help, it is far from sufficient.

As everyone except training companies knows, "informal" learning is what really enables people to acquire new skills and improve their performance at work. The single largest driver is experience, of course: We learn best by doing.

The most important knowledge and skills that we need to perform in a job are acquired on the job in communities of practice. We look and learn from others; we call on people in our network to explain how things work; and we naturally gravitate to those subject matter experts who are generous with their expertise.

Does this mean that the family security manager doesn't need to do anything special to ensure that people learn on the job? Hardly.

...and the role of the family security manager

Family security managers are instrumental in establishing both the formalized training and the informal learning that enables staff to learn and grow. If they aren't living and breathing this responsibility every day, they aren't doing their jobs.

Good managers seize every chance to create learning and development opportunities. Instead of saving everything for a yearly review, they'll make use of even a little downtime to learn more about their staff's developmental interests and career goals.

Once a detail is completed and it's time for an after-action review, they'll ask simple questions like "What are the lessons learned?" When they plan a new detail, they'll consider – and inquire into – how individual agents can contribute and what they'd like to learn. What it would take to bump the person up a notch in terms of responsibility?

The learning-oriented manager always makes it a point to keep everyone on the team informed of the big picture. What's going on in the organization that can impact our work? Where are the best practices that can inspire us to do better? How are others embodying the values that we want to inform our work?

As family security managers, we need to take learning and development seriously

Think back on the teachers you had while growing up, and you'll probably remember one or two with particular fondness. Do the same with the list of managers you've had throughout your career. Some will stand out as people who have been instrumental in helping you make career progress.

We've all met them. We need more of them in the family se-curity industry.

Chapter 15:
Make or buy? Some considerations concerning security for high net worth individuals and family offices

The "make-or-buy" decision is a classic quandary for manufacturing companies. Is the corporation better off making a product or component, or would it be smarter to buy the product from an external supplier?

Also called "the outsourcing question", the same issues apply when high net worth families and individuals are faced with the choice of developing in-house service capabilities or contracting with an external service provider: Should they hire their own staff – including security managers, agents, and security drivers – or should they outsource this work to a partner that specializes in executive protection and residential security?

Family offices tasked with implementing a security program often face this decision with little to guide them. We encourage those responsible for such decisions to consider the same tools used by procurement experts to answer the outsourcing question when performing make-or-buy analyses.

Make-or-buy analyses employ four key criteria

There are dozens of make-or-buy decision models and no self-respecting consultancy is without its own "unique" take on how to address this perennial question.

A quick glance across many models, however, reveals four basic criteria that practically all decisions are based on – or should be:

- *Cost efficiency:* What are the total costs of making or buying the given service?

- *Core competence:* Are the competencies necessary to deliver the services core to the corporation's strategy and success?

- *Performance capability:* How difficult is it to develop the necessary capabilities and can we perform as well as industry leaders?

- *Risks:* What are the risks associated with both insourcing and outsourcing the service?

1. Cost efficiency

When considering the costs of protection programs, it is imperative to include all direct and indirect costs, over time, to arrive at a reliable evaluation of total costs of program ownership.

Direct costs are straightforward, consisting largely of salaries for protective personnel. Other direct costs may include subcontracting secure travel vendors in foreign territories, vehicles, and communication equipment.

Indirect costs are also primarily related to program staff. These include all expenses associated with recruitment, training, bonuses, benefits, turn-over, terminations, etc.

One important note on costs concerns distinguishing between what the principal or family office pays and what the principal's employer might pay. Does the family office pay only for costs that cover residential protection and protection of the principal's family members? Does the employer pay for costs that cover work-related security?

Often, security for individuals and families is paid for by both family offices and corporations. This can present the family office as well as the corporation with accounting and organizational challenges – and lead to gaps in security for the principal. The utilization of a specialist partner provides seamless protection services regardless of whether the corporation or its employee is footing the bill. Costs can be more easily segregated between business and personal use when a specialist partner provides services.

2. Core competence

Executive protection, residential security, and security driving do not belong to the core competencies of any family office or Fortune 500 corporation, and this has particular implications for the HR function. Most corporations prefer not to use headcount or dedicate HR expertise to such non-core, specialized services. Some family offices do, while others don't.

While the safety and productivity of the corporation's leading principals are important, of course, the talent required to provide these will rarely rank very high on the corporate HR department's list of priorities. To staff and run an executive protection program on its own, the corporation would need to become experts in sourcing, interviewing, security screening, training and developing, compensating, on-boarding and off-boarding executive protection managers and agents – just to mention a few HR issues.

In our experience, the same applies to family offices.

It is not enough to choose someone to start or run a family protection program solely based on a career in governmental protection, law enforcement, or the military. Although many tactical skills are similar, the strategies, rules, tools and cultures are completely different, and there can be a long and arduous ramp up time. Choosing someone who has never built or managed a family security program is fraught with risk. It is not fair to the principals, the individual being hired, or the family office, and sets them all up for frustration, disillusionment, and failure.

There is a belief that a full-time employee doing security work will have more loyalty and dedication to keeping principals safe than an outsourced provider. Our experience begs us to differ.

Professional security is not a standard function within any family office. Agents have limited opportunities for career development. Studies have shown that employees value a good working environment, professional challenges, and opportunities for advancement over straight compensation. We also know that motivation wanes after doing the same thing for an extended period of time. This can lead to complacency and a drop off in discipline which, in turn, reduces the effectiveness of risk mitigation. Specialist security companies are more likely than family offices to provide industry-competitive salaries, 401k's, benefit packages, development/mentoring opportunities and career advancement.

There is also a belicf shared by some security agents that working for a "vendor" or "contractor" is a much riskier than being a full-time employee of a family office. In our experience, security agents who are family office full-time equivalent employees face the risks of job stagnation and dismissal without the support and mentoring of a specialist partner.

Full time employees can and do get dismissed just as any outsourced person. Depending on the reason for dismissal, outsourced individuals employed by a specialist partner are likely to have other opportunities within the company. When, as often happens, the reason for dismissal is that the person is not a "good fit", a specialist partner can help employees find a place where they are a "good fit". Specialist partners are also better equipped to identify and help fix an employee's shortcomings than a family office – ideally BEFORE there is a need for dismissal.

A specialist partner company depends on the success of its employees for its own success. They are part of a larger team. They have advisors who know the work and its pitfalls, and they can call for help when they run into an unfamiliar situation. Employees of a specialist partner working for a family office have a team of experienced people in their corner that are directly invested in their success.

Specialist partner providers have a vested interest and experience in finding candidates that have the best chance for long-term success. They appreciate the need for developing people and skills and are accustomed to ensuring that all agents have an annual training program including drills, tabletops, and recurring basic training to keep perishable skills fresh. They can provide advanced development training designed to increase agent capabilities and performance quality. And they know the importance of spotting talent and encouraging the best to follow career paths of growing expertise and responsibility.

Specialist partners have a deep bench of pre-screened and vetted candidates for security agent and manager positions. If one does not work out – for whatever reason – they can be changed quickly and efficiently. What is more, they have immediate access to a worldwide professional network of closely-vetted vendors, enabling them to provide complementary services, quickly and globally.

3. Performance capability

Specialist partners are, well, specialists.

Their management teams have hands-on experience in corporate and family protection that can be decades long. They have operating procedures that have proven their worth in practice. They know how to recruit and develop agents who go on to have success. They can transfer skills learned working for one family office to another. They have experience in communicating about service levels and program value. And they know how to deal with common misconceptions and push-back from stakeholders unfamiliar with these services.

Unlike a family office that is building its own protection program from scratch, specialist partners which serve many clients can benchmark against other programs. They have a hard-earned sense of what constitutes best industry practice. And they bring this to their clients in many ways, from program design and implementation to full or partial staffing.

Specialist partners enable speedy implementation and adaptation. A specialist partner can implement in less than 48 hours what would take an inexperienced family office months to accomplish: Put in place a fully functional protection program that keeps the principals safe, happy and productive wherever their personal interests or jobs take them. Given the backdrop of why we do what we do – often tangible threats to the principal's wellbeing – fast program implementation can be a necessity, not a luxury.

Specialist partners are also able to respond rapidly to evolving program needs. Should the program need to be scaled up, domestically or internationally, to cover other principals or residences, or to provide more protection in more places, this can be done without lengthy onboarding and training processes. Other services such as event security, secure travel logistics, and intelligence analysis can be added immediately.

Similarly, if the program should need to be scaled back for whatever reason, then this can be done straight away and without concern for severance compensation.

4. Risks

The biggest single risk facing family offices that hire their own security staff is that of being sued by former or current disgruntled employees. Although there are a number of highly publicized cases of this, these are but the tip of the iceberg. Unfortunately, this is far more common than most people realize.

Family offices using protective services need to protect themselves against such legal liabilities. Unlike in corporate contexts where principals are differently insulated from legal claims, high net worth individuals face a number of potential legal challenges from current and former protective employees that can result in both unwanted media coverage and substantial settlements.

Some examples of lawsuits and other legal difficulties that involve protective personnel and their employers:

- *Hostile work environments:* Home environments can be as tough as they are wonderful.

- *Work environments with illegal substances:* Protective employees that accompany principals and/or family members that use illegal drugs, or whose underage children use alcohol, are liable to legal prosecution and may, in turn, hold their employers liable for putting them at this risk.

- *Work environments with sexual harassment and/or discrimination:* It can happen anywhere, and close protection situations are clearly no exception. Even before the #metoo and #timesup movements, a number of high-profile cases have been brought against celebrities by former protective personnel.

- *Violations of labor laws:* Although protecting high net worth families might seem more glamorous than other jobs, work is work according to labor laws in most jurisdictions. Not paying for overtime, misclassification of employment status (salaried versus hourly) and meal/rest break violations – just to mention a few – have all resulted in unfortunate lawsuits.

In the majority of these cases, disgruntled employees enabled by ambitious lawyers are looking for money to right a perceived wrong. Sometimes their beefs are quite legitimate, sometimes less so. It does not always matter, as families typically settle out of court, often at considerable cost, to avoid the reputational wrecking ball of high-profile court cases.

As we pointed out in Chapter 6, there are also risks relating to licensing issues with which family offices normally have no experience. Hiring an ex- or off-duty law enforcement officer who is able to carry weapons legally has its own complications in private security work.

Use of force is by no means an everyday occurrence for protection professionals. To the contrary, good programs go a long way to prevent situations where force is necessary, relying on forward thinking more than reactive measures. Still, using specialist partners can reduce the individual and family's legal exposure and eliminate the need for special licensing and insurance coverage. Professional security companies will have their own use of force policies, potentially obviating the family office's need for such.

The business of protecting individuals and families is by its very nature up close and personal. Relationships are complex, sensitive and impactful – especially when they go wrong. Understanding the relational pitfalls of family protection programs significantly reduces the risk of principal dissatisfaction/frustration, program hiccups, and failure.

Favoritism of one agent over others leads to over reliance on that agent, big headedness, and eventual burnout. The risk is real, and inexperienced family offices are more likely to run into it than seasoned specialist partners.

Because protection agents spend a lot of time in the immediate proximity of the principals, small things can have a large impact. Personality traits and mannerisms aren't necessarily right or wrong. Still, personality is plenty of reason to ask for another protective agent or even to dismiss one. Protection programs constantly risk failure due to close scrutiny of their performance not only by the principals. As we saw in the story of Tom, personal frictions can also arise with other estate staff.

If the principal becomes dissatisfied with a manager or agent for whatever reason, this might compromise the program and the principal's security. It is therefore imperative that the principal not hesitate, due to respect for the security agent's feelings or fear of legal action, to terminate the person with whom he or she is not comfortable.

From one-off projects to comprehensive programs: Flexibility is key

When it comes to security program staffing, family offices tackle the make-buy issue in many ways. But we do see some similarities.

One-off and special projects, such as taking care of a principal on business trips to selected destinations or event security, usually rely on outsourced resources.

Similarly, new residential security and security driver programs are typically started by companies hired by the family office, as are more comprehensive programs initially, since family offices have neither the expertise nor other resources to establish the program on their own. This will typically include consulting on program setup, outsourced executive protection agents and/or residential security agents, and an outsourced security manager.

As the program matures, some family offices may choose to make the security protection manager their own full-time employee, with or without consulting support from a specialist partner. Doing so squarely places the security function within the family office's organizational chart. Some executive protection and residential security agents may also become full-time employees, while others will be outsourced in an embedded capacity.

Embedding executive protection and residential security agents, managers, and possibly intelligence analysts has its own advantages. These persons live and breathe in the family office ecosystem but also have the benefits of being able to draw on the specialist partner's network of expertise. Fully mature family office security programs are often a hybrid of own their full-time employees and employees embedded from a specialist partner.

Chapter 16:
How to write an RFP for protective services

Every good security program starts with a good request for proposal (RFP). Or should, at least. Because the RFP is the most powerful document the family office has to structure the bidding process and improve the transparency of competing bidders' advantages and disadvantages.

All organizations have their own purchasing policies and procedures, and most will probably already have guidelines and templates regarding RFPs. But few family offices have much experience in outsourcing such a specialist partner service as executive protection. Given the family security protection program's close-up-and-personal visibility with the principals, this experience gap matters.

In this chapter, we provide an outline of the various elements a good RFP should contain. It will allow family offices to organize RFPs, clarify the decision criteria they will apply in choosing specialist security partners, and ask the right questions to make an informed decision.

Price is inevitably one of the most scrutinized of all the many criteria, and of course it matters. But we would encourage organizations to broaden the scope of the RFP well beyond price. We've been called in to fix a number of programs that started out with low-cost vendors but ended up costing far more than they should have. In security like anything else, you get what you pay for. But unlike many other purchases, the costs of a failed security program can be much greater than purely financial.

Scoring and weighting according to well defined decision criteria

We think it's a good idea to lay out the decision criteria in clusters, weight each of them according to relative importance, then score your evaluation of each vendor bid, for example, as in the table below. It's also a good idea to inform vendors of your criteria and how you intend to weight them.

Criteria	Weight	A	B	C
Company background/management	10			
Protective service capabilities	10			
Human resource management	20			
Protective service processes	20			
Implementation plan	10			
Reference	10			
Price	20			
Total	**100**			

How you choose and weight these decision criteria is an individual matter, and even careful scoring won't allow you to delegate the decision to a numerical model. Personal chemistry and gut feelings do matter. But we hope this chapter will enable you to move beyond the "I know a guy" method to a more effective – and ultimately successful – way of choosing a specialist partner in this niche field.

Statement of Work/Scope of Work

The statement of work (SOW) should make clear just what kinds of protective services the family office wants to contract. But realistically, it can be difficult or impossible for family offices with no experience in protective services to know exactly what they need.

How extensive does the Risk, Threat, and Vulnerability Analysis (RTVA) need to be? How often should it be updated? Are advance trips to upcoming travel destinations always necessary? Why or why not? Should intelligence analysis be part of the program?

Answers to these and many more questions can be elusive for non-experts. That's why some corporations and family offices rely on external consultants to carry out an RTVA and make SOW recommendations based on the results.

The SOW should cover at least all the basic points listed below:

- **Who:** Principal(s) to be protected
- **What:** Specific tasks
  - o   Threat assessments
  - o   Residential security
  - o   Security driving

- o   Close protection
- o   Secure travel logistics and advance work
- **When:** Full time, part time
- **Where:**
  - o   Office
  - o   Residential
  - o   Travel
  - o   Domestic
  - o   International
- **How:**
  - o   Specific tasks
  - o   Procedures
  - o   Operational planning
  - o   Staffing and training
  - o   SOPs
  - o   Quality control/KPIs
  - o   Reporting
  - o   Contingency/response plans
  - o   Stakeholder communication
  - o   Expense reporting and invoicing
  - o   Personnel and program evaluation
  - o   Key personnel needed from vendor

Vendor background information

Once you have defined the scope of work, you're ready to start asking potential vendors to bid on it. The next thing to do is to get vendors to provide information that will let you evaluate their expertise and ultimately let you choose among them.

The first cluster of decision criteria lets you examine some of the basics: You need to get some general background information from all vendors.

Financial information: Ask all bidders to provide information that proves their company is a viable business. Are they profitable? Are they growing? Can you count on them to be around in a year? To find out, you should go back at least three years and require seeing at least the balance sheet and income statement.

Management team: Good companies have good management – also in the security industry. Ask for the management team's bios or CVs. Find out which person at the senior executive level will be accountable for your program. If the scope of work calls for a team or onsite manager, you'll also want to learn more about who the vendor proposes for this important role.

Mission, values, and guiding principles: Try to move beyond all the marketing talk and get a good sense of what makes the vendor tick. What kind of values do they try to instill throughout their company? Do they have a set of guiding principles that are clear and actionable? Do they walk the talk?

Compliance with ethical, environmental, and other corporate purchasing guidelines: Be sure to ask about whatever is relevant for your family office. Some of the more common guidelines include:

- *Quality control:* What kinds of quality assurance programs does the vendor use? Are they certified according to ISO 9000 or 9001 standards?

- *Non-discrimination:* How does the vendor ensure compliance with non-discrimination policies regarding gender, race, etc.? For larger programs, how can they ensure that the diversity of the national workforce is also reflected in the protective team?

- *Environmental:* Does the vendor comply with agreed environmental standards? What kinds of certifications does it use to ensure compliance?

- *Anti-corruption/bribery:* What are the vendor's policies regarding corruption, bribery, etc.? For example, do managers and agents receive training in the UK Bribery Act or other accepted ways of preventing bribery?

- *Global presence:* If the individual or family lifestyle includes foreign travel, then a potential vendor's global presence is a relevant criterion. Seamless quality of service regardless of location is a hallmark of good protection, and you will want to understand the vendor's ability to provide protection and smooth logistics worldwide.

This is worth considering even if the scope of work currently calls for protection in only one country, which is exceedingly rare in our globalized economy. Protection needs change, sometimes quickly; you want your family protection vendor to scale internationally as and when necessary.

Ask to learn more about the vendors:

- *Own locations:* Where do they have people, offices or subsidiaries?

- *Vetted vendor/partner locations:* Where do they have tested, tried and true partners?

- *Vendor vetting procedures:* What are their procedures for selecting, training and briefing other companies in other territories? How do they carry out remote supervision? How do you know the "security driver" they provide in Karachi is reliable, and that you can safely entrust your principal to his driving skills and background?

- **Insurance:** How is the vendor's liability and other insurance coverage? Be sure to get some insight into the kind and level of insurance protection.

- **Licensing:** Licensing requirements vary internationally and by state in the U.S. Ask vendors to provide information on what kinds of licenses allow it to operate where.

Vendor protective service capabilities

When choosing a security provider, it's important to gain a comprehensive overview of the bidding vendors' capabilities. That they all can build and deliver a basic residential security program should be a given, so you will as a minimum want to examine their expertise concerning protective agents, security drivers and program management.

In order to future-proof your vendor relationship, however, it is a good idea to look beyond the minimum requirements. You need to ask questions about related security services, too.

- Can they provide you with strategic planning support in addition to tactical implementation?

- Do they have experience in family protection programs? How do they recommend aligning executive protection services with the rest of the security program?

- If the need arises, can they ramp up security with protective surveillance or counter surveillance teams?

- What is their track record in adding intelligence analysis to protective programs? How would they recommend staffing, managing and integrating the intel piece into the overall program?

- Can they also provide event security? Depending on the family's needs, it might make good business sense to ask the same vendor to handle residential protection and event security services.

When considering all of these protective service capabilities, it important to consider vendors as long-term partners with whom you will be building and maintaining the program. Unlike other security services, protection is intimately entwined with the principal's daily routines and lifestyle. Once implemented, there is a resistance to making major changes, so choosing the best partner from the beginning is even more important here than in other areas with less direct involvement with the principal.

Human resource management

Personal security is a people business: While this is true for many industries, the close-up-and-personal nature of family protection makes human resource management an especially critical decision criterion. The RFP process should enable the family office to understand how vendors manage HR because a provider's ability to recruit, develop and retain the best people is essential to program success.

Scope: The first thing to look at is the kinds of employees the vendor can provide. Depending on the nature of the program, you may need to fill some or all of the jobs listed below, and you want to be sure that your vendor has the necessary experience and expertise in providing quality people. How do they recruit, vet, develop and retain these specialists?

- Residential security agents
- Security drivers
- Executive protection agents
- Protective surveillance agents
- Security managers
- Intelligence analysts
- Event security specialists

Vetting process: You should ask tough questions about how the vendor vets potential candidates for each job type. What policies and procedures do they follow in order to ensure that those charged with protecting the principal are worthy of this trust?

"Background checks" can be bought off the shelf, and some vendors are satisfied with low-cost but superficial versions of these. Others have far more thorough processes that might include anything from extensive and recurring reference checks to social media analyses and even polygraph tests.

Hard skills and experience: A variety of trainable, demonstrable skills is essential to good security protection. These vary according to the specific job type.

You will want to understand how the vendor sets standards for training and experience for each and every job type called for in the scope of work:

- What are the minimum training qualifications for each job type? Which courses must candidates have completed? From which type of training school?

- How many years of relevant experience are necessary for each job type?

- Ask to see job descriptions and required qualifications for each job type.

- What are the providers' policies for refreshing perishable skills? For many skill sets, including critical ones like evasive driving and emergency medical care, it's use it or lose it: Providers who aren't requiring their staff to do regular training aren't doing their job.

- Certifications: Does the vendor have company-wide quality assurance certifications such as ISO 9001? What kinds of certifications are necessary to fulfill specific job types?

Soft skills: As we point out in Part IV, the mastery of hard skills is a necessary but insufficient qualification for success in a family security protection job. Emotional intelligence is equally important. Why? Because unless the people providing the protection thoroughly understand and adapt to the principal's personal preferences, it is unlikely that the program will achieve sustainable success.

To thrive in family protection, agents, drivers, and managers must possess a variety of characteristics we call "soft skills". To mention a few: resilience, empathy, discretion, and self-awareness. While dedicated effort can improve all of these, they are essentially personality traits that some people possess more than others.

The context of the RFP is too narrow to investigate the psychological makeup of potential agents. Still, it is a good opportunity to discover how seriously vendors take this critical aspect of the business, so at least a few good questions are in order:

- What are the provider's procedures for ensuring good cultural fit between the principals, protective agents, and other estate or family office stakeholders? What do they actually do to adapt programs accordingly?

- How does the provider make sure that the program meets the principal's personal preferences? What are their procedures for discovering these, and for making sure they are respected across three-shift teams and around the world if necessary?

- What procedures does the provider use to evaluate the soft skills of its candidates? How does it match individual agents and managers to individual clients?

Employee continuity: The security industry is notorious for high staff turnover and low employee loyalty. This has negative consequences for the quality of its services and for the reputation of the entire industry.

For far too many years, the industry has failed to give our employees the means to develop their careers. We have not been good enough at nurturing talent through career planning, and we have paid the price: Too many high performers have switched companies to climb up a rung of the career ladder and too many low performers have stayed where they are.

While it's not the family office's headache to organize a supplier's HR efforts, if it is interested in sustainable program success, it will want to enquire how the vendor does so. Be sure to ask how the vendor ensures staff continuity through employee retention and career planning. Two simple metrics that are useful: employee turnover rate and average years of employment.

Employee compensation and benefits: It is a fair question in the RFP process to ask how the vendor pays its employees. Transparency around employee compensation and benefits (including 401k, health, life, vision, dental, short-term disability, long-term disability, paid time off, performance bonuses, etc.) is important. Because everything else being equal, vendors who provide competitive salary and benefit packages are more likely to attract the best talent. We have yet to work for a client who doesn't want the best talent when it comes to protection.

Scalability/surge capacity: Extending program scope may mean adding resources, and family offices need to consider vendors' ability to scale up quickly if this becomes necessary. Adding another principal to the program could effectively double the staff needed. Can the vendor respond quickly? How? What kinds of lead times are necessary?

Vendor protective service processes

You will want to pay particular attention to how vendors organize the nuts and bolts of their services. All of the bullet points below are important, and you should ask vendors to provide information on the procedures and processes they use for all of them.

Who does what? When and with what frequency? How do they actually do it? What information do they supply? What is expected of you in each process? Where will you need to approve or review?

- Risk, Threat, and Vulnerability Analysis (RTVA)
- Operational planning
- Staffing and training
- Standard operating procedures (SOPs)
- Quality control/key performance indicators (KPIs)
- Reporting
- Contingency/response plans
- Stakeholder communication
- Expense reporting and invoicing
- Personnel and program evaluation

All of the above points are important, but we want to call out one in particular: *reporting*.

Like any other expense the family office commits to, security is an investment that will be scrutinized in many ways. Security managers can be hard-pressed to demonstrate the return on investment of a protection program: If nothing happened to the principals either before or after program implementation, then what difference has the program made?

Good reporting based on solid data can help security managers quantify program value. You should ask vendors to tell what kind of data they can and will report, how they will do it, and with what frequency.

Implementation plan

A great way to learn how a company works is to ask them to describe how they would implement the new program. What are the process milestones? When can you expect these to be achieved? Who on the vendor side will be involved – and who on the corporate side will need to be involved?

References

Last but by no means least are client references.

Have the vendors provided similar services for similar clients? How did things go? Are they still providing services? Why or why not?

Go beyond the simple client list. Ask to contact one or more of the family offices they work for directly, so you can learn firsthand of their experiences with, and opinion of, the vendor.

Price schedule

Ask vendors to break down all costs so that you can see how they arrive at a total – and compare competing bids at the line-item level.

Be sure to capture all costs – both fixed and variable, ongoing, out of pocket, etc., and to understand what is and is not included in the budget.

RFP Schedule/Timing

Depending on the complexity of the scope of work, the RFP process can take anywhere from a week to several months.

Be sure to allocate adequate time for vendors and the purchasing department to prepare and complete the steps below:

1. Issue request for proposal
2. Requests for clarification due
3. Response to request for clarification due
4. Notice of intent to bid due
5. Proposal due date
6. Oral presentations
7. Expected contract start date

Part III:
Transitions in family
protective security

Introduction to Part III: Change management in protective security for families – start-up, turnaround, realign or sustain?

Changes in family programs are inevitable. As Benjamin Franklin noted centuries ago, "When you're finished changing, you're finished". For managers of family protection programs and other stakeholders, understanding the changes we face at various program pivot points is crucial.

Part III examines the key transitions that family security programs are likely to face at one time or another. To do so, we borrow from Michael Watkins of IMD, who has written extensively on managing business and career transitions. He provides some actionable insights that can also be applied to the changes that are typical in family security programs. We've taken the liberty of tweaking Watkins's five-pointed STAR model down to the four transitions that are most relevant for family protection programs:

- Start-up
- Turnaround
- Realignment
- Sustaining success

For those tasked with managing family security programs, much of Watkins's solid advice holds true across all four transitions. This includes the necessity of aligning program changes with family protection strategies, relentless focus on key priorities, and the importance of early wins.

Our focus will be on the first two transitional phases – startup and turnaround – as these are the most relevant for most family offices. We will then briefly deal with the challenges of realigning a program that, while not currently in distress, will be headed for trouble unless there is a change in course, as well as how to sustain a high-performance program. Finally, we will examine another all too common transition that affects many family security programs: the changes wrought by separation and divorce.

We begin Part III with the story of Paul, a protective agent who got a lot of things right but got one thing very wrong. As we will see, Paul's penchant to play favorites – facilitated by the principals and his team – led to his downfall after divorce changed the dynamics of the family's protection program.

The story of Paul

Paul was a bright young protective agent working for a husband-and-wife pair of principals. For her own reasons, the wife thought Paul was the best agent on the team and considered him her favorite agent. Whenever possible, she made sure it was Paul who drove her wherever she needed to go and provided protection for her at public events. This occurred so regularly that both the team and the principal's husband couldn't help but notice.

The husband paid it no mind and was, in fact, supportive, happy that his wife had Paul with her. Paul wasn't experienced enough to realize that he should have downplayed the favorite card instead of pushing it. He began to do everything in his power to make sure he stayed the wife's preferred agent, even if this hurt the team and their overall purpose. For example, he held back information on the wife's preferences, so his fellow agents wouldn't be aware of details such as how she preferred doors to be opened, where to put the gum and mints in the car, and how close she wanted coverage in public. In her mind, the other agents just weren't as competent as Paul. So, after a while, Paul got what he wanted: He was her favorite and went everywhere with her.

Although the rest of the team did not respect him for playing favorites, he did have the favor of the principals, at least for a while. This, too, changed when the principals' marriage began to unravel.

The husband was unhappy and started engaging in extra-marital activities with a number of women. Things became awkward for the husband when Paul was on coverage. Although the husband liked Paul, it was Paul, after all, who was his wife's favorite. Was Paul more loyal to him or to his wife? Could Paul be counted on to show discretion despite the principal's marital indiscretions?

Paul began to feel the awkwardness, too. He saw what the husband was doing outside the marriage, and although he did his best to remain neutral and keep out of the principal's business, he sensed the husband's waning trust. Things became even more awkward when the wife complained about her marriage to her friends while Paul was standing by on coverage.

The principals eventually took a trial separation, and the wife moved to the beach house. One night shortly after the move, the wife called the command post and Paul answered. She had been trying in vain to reach her husband, but he didn't pick up. "I know he doesn't want to talk to me, but can you please make him take my phone call?"

Ever the favorite, Paul promised to try to accommodate the wife's wishes – knowing fully well that the principal was entertaining his mistress and had explicitly asked to not be disturbed. Thinking on his feet, Paul explained the situation to the principal's personal assistant and routed the wife to her, so he could avoid being put in the middle of both principals. The executive assistant handled the situation as the principal wanted, saying he was unavailable, and that she would relay the message to the principal. That was a close call, but Paul thought he had dodged a bullet.

Unfortunately, the marriage continued to disintegrate. When Paul worked with the wife, she'd ask him all kinds of questions about her husband's activities and whereabouts. Whereas Paul had always engaged with her in polite, friendly banter (more than he should have), he now felt the pressure to choose sides. He did his best to stay impartial and not share any information, but this deviated from the previously cozy chattiness he shared with the wife. It was very difficult for Paul to change the dynamic of the relationship from favored son to neutral outsider. Paul knew he was in trouble.

Once the divorce finally occurred, the security team was split between the husband and the wife, with the husband getting most team members and the wife just a few. Paul was not asked to join the wife's team because she didn't feel close to him anymore, and he stayed on with the husband.

A few months after the divorce the husband decided he didn't want to have Paul around anymore. Every time he saw Paul, it reminded him of his ex-wife. Her favorite agent was no longer a favorite, and he was no longer needed. Paul ended up losing his job because he had played the favorite instead of playing his cards right. When the family transitioned from married to divorced, he did not make the transition.

Favoritism is an easy trap to fall into for principals as well as agents. It must be avoided.

Chapter 17:
Starting up a family security program

Every family security program starts somewhere. And although a number of prominent families and high net worth individuals do already use protection, a significant segment still does not. Navigating the start-up phase of an individual or family protection program is particularly tricky for many security directors and would-be principals: They're simply not familiar with family protection, and they're starting from scratch.

The transitions

This chapter addresses the process of moving from no-protection program to a working program – even at a small scale. Additions to or expansions of an existing program, e.g., adding a new principal, a new estate, or a new program dimension, can in many ways also be considered as "startups".

Protection programs for high net worth individuals and families often evolve from simple to complex, from part time to full time. For example, protection may begin with a residential security assessment or secure travel services for an individual principal, then expand to include residential security for one or more residences, then add additional principals as families grow. Or, programs might start with residential security only in certain circumstances, such as heightened concerns about persons of interest, then add more coverage, then eventually turn into 24/7 protection.

Similarly, programs can begin with "the basics", e.g., a Risk, Threat, and Vulnerability Analysis (RTVA) that results in part- or full time...

- Residential security agents

- Secure drivers

- Close protection agents...

...then evolve to include more "advanced" program dimensions such as:

- Part-or full-time intelligence analysts

- Security operations centers, on- or off-premises

- Event security

- Surveillance detection

- Covert protection

Key objectives

1. Get a security program running where there has been none

2. Integrate a new security service into an existing program

Key milestones

Recognition of need: The individual or family decides that a professional security program or additional service is necessary, feasible and a sound investment – and selects a provider.

Program design: The provider defines the processes and the capabilities that will make it happen.

Initial implementation: Deliver a first impression of operational excellence – even if this is more of a "baby step" than a giant leap forward.

Key challenges

The principal's, family's, (and possibly, the security director's) lack of experience with professional protection: Most often, families new to professional protection have no idea of their relative prominence or how this prominence impacts security, no security expertise, no baseline of "this is how we usually do it", and no opportunity to compare with others. There may be no one on staff with any practical protection insight; often, there is no family security director, and the principal's corporation might be asked to set up the program.

Unfortunately, however, preconceived notions and misconceptions about protective security abound. Although a security director might have a clear idea about the differences between professional close protection and "bodyguards", the principal and his or her family may not. Understandably, most principals with no protection experience will easily confuse the tabloid images of intrusive bodyguards with the reality of well-trained close protection agents. They will quickly pull up the same pictures of close protection as the general population: Hollywood stars walking behind a phalanx of muscle-bound men in black;

scruff-ups with paparazzi; insensitive indiscretions and tell-all book deals.

Thus, an important challenge when initiating a protection program for the principal and the family is ignorance of what executive protection actually is (and isn't). Since it is often the case that everyone involved in a new family security program will have to reassess their conception of executive protection, one of our most important tasks in the start-up phase is communicating clearly about the actual nature of a professional family security program and actual value.

It is helpful to approach the startup of a new program in an iterative way, where the principal and providers stay in close contact through the initial steps of program initiation in order to dial in the most appropriate program incrementally.

Building the family security network from scratch requires close coordination with many stakeholders: Unless the principal is used to professional protection as part of the job, a brand-new family protection program will have no established network to rely on, so every connection to every stakeholder will have to be created and nurtured. Inclusion of and coordination with all relevant elements of the family office ecosystem, as described in Chapter 4, are essential challenges to be overcome.

Family office accounting managers need to understand a new category of costs: It is essential that family office accounting managers have a good understanding of what drives costs - and who's paying for what. For example, when the principal's travel plans change, as they can from week to week, this impacts the variable costs of a family security program due to the advance trips, travel expenses, and agent hours needed to accommodate every new itinerary. So, if the budget was based on 10 trips in a given period, and the family ends up making more or fewer trips, there will be a discrepancy between planned and actual costs. Does that mean the family should not take the trips they need to take, or that they should only get security on budgeted trips? Probably not.

Another issue for accountants is making clear distinctions between what a principal's company pays for and what the principal's family office pays for. In theory, it's simple: Business costs are paid by the company; personal costs are paid by the family office. In practice, there can be a lot of gray between the black and white. Full transparency and proactive dialogue go a long way to prevent problems and address them quickly, if necessary. This applies to those responsible for accounting and to those responsible for running both corporate and personal security programs.

Customizing the security program to individual or family preferences: One of the keys to a successful program start is understanding as much as possible about client preferences in order to customize the security program accordingly. Cookie cutter solutions are rarely sustainable for high net worth individuals who are accustomed to arranging the circumstances of their lives according to their wishes rather than simply grabbing a standard solution off the shelf.

To customize client-facing aspects of the security program, a number of guided conversations with the principals and/or their representatives must occur. These conversations cover a range of topics that can usually be done in person if you have the time – or written depending on time. They cover a lot of areas that the principals and/or their representatives just might not think about and gets them on your side immediately because they'll see that you're covering every base. Some of those conversational topics might, for example, include:

- What does the family like or dislike about security? Any pet peeves to understand and work around?

- Should a residential security program attempt to minimize the visibility of security from young children for as long as possible, and present agents as drivers and helpers rather than armed guards? Should covert protection be part of the mix? How should security agents and drivers deal with the things that teenagers do and don't do?

- What level of involvement and direct communication between the family and security is appropriate? What is the preferred chain of command? What decisions should the security team make on its own, and what should they seek guidance on?

- Are there areas of the estate or residence that are off limits for security? For example, some principals will establish something like a "red zone" (master bed/bath, private house, etc.) where no staff or security are allowed while they're on property, but that turns into a "green zone" when the family goes off site.

- Should we introduce code words and safe phrases, special phrases which, when communicated by the principal or the security team, will convey problems and issues? For example, if the principal is feeling overwhelmed in a crowd looking for photos or autographs, they can say something like, "Can we get a sandwich, please?", so protection agents know that the principal has had enough, and the agents need to step in. Something similar can apply if the agents sense there is a problem and want to move the principal to another location.

HR needs to hire new kinds of employees: Family offices may or may not have a dedicated HR function. It is extremely unlikely that they have any experience recruiting, developing and retaining staff within the niche domain of high-end security – or how to build and maintain an effective security organization.

Staffing levels must be correct from the start or soon become so. Applying cookie-cutter staffing policies and procedures to family security agents who might be called on to work 80-hour weeks and spend more time on the road than at home will have its own consequences.

Another HR issue is training: Even well-trained protection agents are only as good as their readiness, and readiness depends on constantly keeping complacency at bay. Some protection skills are perishable, and while HR departments new to executive protection may find courses in, for example, emergency driving, more "nice to have" than "need to have", this unfamiliarity with protection best practices and staffing needs should not be allowed to impinge on the program's overall effectiveness.

Reporting lines and decision-making authority can be opaque: In the corporate world, even in convoluted matrix organizations, employees are seldom in doubt as to "who is the boss". Family security is different.

Whereas most CEOs will defer to the chain of command if they notice a lower-level company employee who needs to be nudged, reprimanded, or ultimately replaced, if the principal (or someone in his or her family) doesn't like a family security protection agent – for whatever reason – personal preferences trump organizational hierarchy every time.

The roles and responsibilities of many stakeholders concerned with the principal's security must be understood by all and delineated clearly. As we saw in the story of Tom above, there is plenty of room for misunderstanding and friction.

Corporate chief security officers and executive administrative assistants are used to having their say. So are estate managers, family office managers, and security directors. In most cases, however, principals want to deal with one person on all aspects of the security program and other aspects their personal lives – not the politics of folks jockeying for position. Expectations need to be made clear in the beginning.

Important early wins

The first 100 days are crucial for family security directors. As they get a feel for things and grow into their role, so does the family discover what they do and don't like about the new security program. If the security director's first three months are marred by mishaps and misunderstandings, he or she is likely to be replaced. Even if the initial period is a success, the tenure of the first security director is likely to last no more than three to five years.

In light of the challenges we briefly discuss above, a few initial victories clearly emerge for those who are tasked with starting a family security program from scratch.

Acceptance of the need for family security protection: The first must-win battle is gaining approval from principal to provide at least some protection services, somewhere, sometime. It often makes good sense to commence a family security protection program with "baby steps" rather than a full-blown, 24/7/365 program. This gives everyone involved the opportunity to experience firsthand what professional security actually is. If done properly, it also makes clear that family security provides all-important collateral benefits such as improved travel logistics and increased productivity for the principal.

Operational excellence: First impressions matter. Another must-win battle is that of protection quality. It is essential that the principal and the rest of the family office meet only well trained and carefully selected protection agents – always, of course, and especially in the early days of the program. While the program might able to survive a less-than-optimal executive protection agent after running for a while, if the principal's and organization's initial perceptions of program quality are negative, it might be too late to fix the reputation of a program that got off to a bad start.

Relationship building: Creating bridges rather than walls between key stakeholders in the family, estate management, and family office organizations is critical, for without these, the family security program will flounder. To build relationships in a start-up program, protection professionals must realize that they have a double role: Not only must they execute their jobs flawlessly, but they must also develop stakeholder understanding of what good protection is and how it happens. This will involve a lot of explaining, and, not least, relentlessly demonstrating a professional approach throughout the family ecosystem.

Chapter 18:
Turning around a security program that is in trouble

Considering the many challenges of starting up a family security program, it's no wonder that some are more successful than others. Some programs never get off the ground in the first place, while others fail over time. Any number of things can go awry. The wrong people may have been chosen to staff the program. Security managers might engage poorly with agents, the family ecosystem, or both. There may be no quality control. Complacency might have become the order of the day, resulting in lackadaisical agents.

However, if a protection program is not performing as expected, this does not mean that its underlying objective – the principal's security – is no longer a priority. Rather than simply terminating the program, what's called for is a turnaround.

The transition

Moving from a dysfunctional or unsatisfactory family security program to one that works – and keeps the principals secure as well as enhances their productivity

Key objectives

Turn a non-performing protection program into a high-performing program

Key milestones

1. Recognition that the family security program is non-performing

2. Correct assessment of the root causes of the problem(s)

3. Create a turnaround plan that prioritizes key issues and improvement steps

4. Focus on early wins

Key challenges

Awareness: The first hurdle to overcome in a turnaround situation is recognizing the need for change. Moving people beyond denial to realize that there are problems – and that changes are needed to correct these – is imperative. Becoming aware of poorly performing security programs can be difficult for non-professionals, however. If nothing happens to the family, it can be tempting to conclude there is nothing wrong with the family's security. Nothing could be further from the truth.

Lack of ongoing training is an indicator of dysfunction, as is too much chumminess between family members and security agents. But while these and more obvious signs that should tip off the casual observer – such as agents who are out of shape physically, sleeping on the job, or whose physical appearance is shabby – determining the technical proficiency of agents is not something non-professionals can do. Nor is evaluating the appropriateness of agreed-upon standard operating procedures (SOPs) or how well SOPs are followed. This is not just a question of checking some simple metrics. Those responsible for a poorly functioning family security program will probably not have a clear way to evaluate success or failure.

A strength, weakness, opportunity, and threat analysis (SWOT) of the program with focus on problem assessment is essential. This could include onsite assessments as well as interviews with the principals, security manager and team members, estate, and family office staff. Diagnostic tools, such as simulating emergency scenarios and asking individual team members what they would do can also be useful: If different agents give different responses, we can assume that their SOP and emergency response training leaves something to be desired. It is often more effective to bring in third-party expertise to conduct these analyses rather than to expect that those responsible for creating the situation will also have the wherewithal to rectify it.

Another challenge can be agreeing on the root causes of the problems. It is essential that the security director, principal, and key family office or estate stakeholders get on the same page before deciding to turn a new leaf.

Prioritizing the most critical pain points: Since a dysfunctional program may suffer from a long list of troubles, it can be tempting to try to fix all of them at once. This is not a good idea.

The turnaround process can be compared to medical triage: Among many wounds and illnesses, we have to assign a degree of urgency to all issues, then tackle them in the optimal sequence. First, stop the bleeding, then start the breathing, protect the wound, and treat for shock.

We must identify the roots of the trouble, then address these aggressively. It is better to hone in on the most critical reasons for the problems affecting the security program and then focus on these relentlessly throughout the turnaround. The turnaround plan should build on solving these few core problems, and early wins should hinge on ameliorating their root causes.

Stabilization: In most cases, the program must go on even while analysis of its problems is taking place: Dropping protection of the principals is not an option. Stabilizing a program while preparing to change it may bring its own challenges.

Creating a vision for the future: In order to be successful, those responsible for the turnaround must paint a clear picture of how the new family security program will look once the root causes of underperformance have been identified and corrected. Giving people a realistic image of the light at the end of the tunnel allows them to embrace a shared vision and to look forward rather than backward.

It is important that the vision be clear and compelling, but not so detailed that the turnaround team paints itself into a corner that may be difficult to get out of as the process continues. As we'll see below, creating unrealistic expectations impinges on trustworthiness.

Building credibility: The program's reputation within the family ecosystem is all-important, and trust in the protection program is one of the hardest things to rebuild once it has been undermined by poor performance. Therefore, managing expectations through thoughtful communication is essential in all protection program turnarounds.

Transparency around the turnaround process is essential. If there is bad news, it should all be broken at once rather than rationing it across weeks or months. New teams have the privilege of starting with a fresh slate: They can acknowledge current and past shortcomings, set a new direction, and move on.

Of course, the new team must make good on its promises in order to build its own credibility. By communicating goals, we know we can achieve – and meeting them – security managers build confidence and put precious credit into the emerging program's reliability account.

Important early wins

Creating consensus on the turnaround plan: Once an analysis is complete, all key stakeholders must be on the same page as to what the core problems are and how the turnaround plan will correct these. Key stakeholders will typically include the principal, estate and/or family office managers, and the family security manager, if there is one.

Reorganizing for success: If the analysis reveals that there is a person or persons who are standing in the way of a successful program turnaround – or who is/are largely responsible for the program's dismal state – then moving quickly to remove these people from the team is important. This could be one or more security agents and/or their manager. Although it's a difficult thing to do, if the analysis indicates that someone is more part of the problem than of the solution, then they should not be allowed to stand in the way of the turnaround. Furthermore, by reorganizing early on, a signal is sent that there is a willingness to make changes – also the tougher ones.

Reporting using relevant metrics: Since turnaround efforts will rely on metrics that are directly related to the pain points that the turnaround is designed to address, it is good idea to begin reporting against these metrics as soon as possible.

The importance of keeping up turnaround momentum

There is a tendency for the people involved in security turnarounds to think that they have completed their job once the program is out of immediate trouble. It's natural to celebrate the pain being over, but the festivities shouldn't last too long.

Even though it's easy to overlook or choose not to deal with other underlying issues which might later disrupt the program, smart managers will keep the turnaround going until all concerns have been faced and dealt with. They won't get trapped by the arrogance that their program is so good that it does not need any adjustments. They will root out bad habits and poor results even if they aren't causing immediate pain. They'll be aware of other problems such as favorites syndrome, complacency, and lack of focus on improvement.

Formalized reviews between the principals, security team, family office and/or estate stakeholders are a good way to keep turned-around programs on track and maintain momentum. These should at least be quarterly, but some relationships require higher frequency to ensure the "unhappiness folder" is kept empty and that the stakeholders feel understood.

Chapter 19:
Realigning a family security program that needs to change course

Sometimes a security program might seem to be running fine but actually be headed for trouble. Unlike a turnaround situation where the program is clearly in crisis, a program in need of realignment may not be marked by obvious signals of distress or urgency for change.

Another situation that we sometimes see, especially in post-turnaround programs, also indicates that realignments are needed. After having fixed a program's most critical pain points, there is a tendency to think the program is out of trouble and to rest on our laurels. But just because a program's weakest elements have been strengthened, this doesn't mean the program is as good as it can be. Good managers will continue to push for improvements to make sure the program is always performing at its very best.

The challenges of a realignment transition make up a kind of middle ground between a turnaround and sustaining a successful program. Some program elements work well; others do not. Nonetheless, the careful observer will see clouds gathering on the horizon and realize that if the program sticks to its present course, significant problems will be inevitable.

If a successful program begins to slip, a realignment could head off the need for a turnaround. If the realignment fails, however, then program turnaround will be the only alternative.

The transition

Make changes in a program in order to readjust the security strategy, deliveries, and culture, and thus bolster program quality in the face of current and anticipated challenges.

Key objectives

Ensure continued program success in spite of predictable factors that will make this more difficult; revitalize a program that is headed for trouble.

Key milestones

1. Building consensus for the need for change

2. Realignment plan with concrete steps

3. Restructuring as needed

Key challenges

Complacency: If nothing ever happens to the principal (and fortunately, it rarely does), and he or she seems fairly happy, then it can be tempting to assume that the protection program is performing well. Tempting, but potentially misguided: The program's underlying strategy, culture, and operations might all be in need of an overhaul, and the principal's well-being heretofore may well be as much a product of chance as of the family protection program's design and execution.

Complacency and the resultant decline in readiness can develop quickly without ongoing quality audits and training. Agents that are not challenged get bored. Maintaining an alert team that responds to changing risks, needs, and environments requires constant management attention.

Outdated protection strategy: Family protection strategies need to be critically reviewed from time to time. For one thing, families change over time. For another, a strategy based on an outdated Risk, Threat, and Vulnerability Analysis (RTVA) is not as useful as it used to be. Protection strategies that remain unchanged in the face of familial, organizational, technological, or market developments are probably no longer serving their original purpose.

There is no reason to create an entirely new protection strategy every year. But ongoing RTVA updates and periodic strategy audits should inform all realignment processes.

Program culture: Over time, all family security programs will develop their own culture. A healthy culture will be characterized by openness, consistent dedication to improvement, the ability to learn from mistakes, resilience in the face of difficulties, and a high degree of personal accountability – just to mention a few attributes. As for unhealthy cultures, that's the stuff of another book. Suffice it to say that entrenched ways of doing things and unspoken rules can be a barrier – as well as a support – to realigning a security program.

Favoritism: One thing we will mention about unhealthy family security protection cultures is favoritism (as in Paul's story). We all want to be liked, and some of us may be more likeable than others in a given situation. But a good protection team does not allow favoritism to get in the way of professionalism. As we have emphasized time and time again, when some relationships between security agents and principals get cozier than others, that's a sure sign of trouble.

Skills gap: A security team that does not have the skills it needs to perform at a high level is one thing. This can be addressed by training, new hires, outsourcing, or other means – and indeed often is part of a realignment strategy.

But a security program in need of realignment could well be in the situation where stakeholders simply don't possess the means of properly auditing and rectifying performance.

Important early wins

Acknowledging the need for change: The most important early win in a realignment transition is making key stakeholders aware that the status quo is not a sustainable option. This can be difficult to achieve without a burning platform. But unless this new awareness forms the basis of the realignment effort, it will be doomed to failure.

Trust based on shared understanding and expectations: As soon as possible, those responsible for program realignment must focus on building trust between all stakeholders through transparent communication. We need to describe how a successfully realigned program will look and what we intend to do to achieve it. We must make clear our priorities, what we are doing, and why we are doing it. And we need to be sure that all relevant stakeholders understand each other – and feel understood.

Tangible changes that are in line with the realignment diagnosis: Programs in need of realignment have strengths as well as weaknesses. Managers should aim for clear changes early on that make the strong stronger, and then fix the weaknesses.

Organizationally, this could mean promoting someone who displays the kind of behavior called for by the new strategy, or demoting or removing someone who does not prove to be willing or able to do so. In terms of policy, tangible changes could reflect new priorities on readiness and training, advance planning, or practically any other aspect of the program. It all depends on the situation.

Chapter 20:
Sustaining an effective family protective security program

It may seem counterintuitive, but even excellent family security programs must be challenged to change in order to stay successful. The best way to do this is to make continuous improvement a cornerstone of the security program and culture.

Unlike the other program transitions described above, changes brought on by continuous improvement efforts are likely to be incremental, not revolutionary. Continuous improvement goals informed by ongoing management follow up and quality audits should be pursued throughout the program – not only in a few parts of it – and they should be focused on personnel as well as processes and innovation.

The transition

Incremental transitions, both large and small, in the form of continuous adjustments and improvements to the security program. Smaller adjustments could include tweaking standard operating procedures (SOPs) and key performance indicator (KPI) alignment, for example, larger adjustments might be changes in personnel or providers.

Key objectives

Keep a high-performing family security protection program on track – and make it even better.

Key milestones

1. Roadmap to structure all continuous improvement processes

2. Creating and using clear metrics, both qualitative and quantitative, that are consistently measured relative to a baseline to determine progress or lack thereof. These metrics should be clearly understood by all stakeholders, and enable evaluation of both "hard" and "soft" issues, from tactical execution to alignment with the principals' preferences.

Key challenges

Developing a high-performance culture: Family security programs with high-performance cultures are easy to recognize but hard to copy. High-performance teams and organizations have cultures to match, and often share a number of characteristics. These include:

- Excellent leadership aligned with the overall organization

- No-fat organizational structure with clear roles and re-sponsibilities

- Ongoing motivation of the organization's engagement in excellence and readiness to change, including a dedication to continuous learning as individuals and as a team

- A strong HR strategy that focuses on recruiting the very best talent for every role, then developing it even further

Comparative analysis and benchmarking: It's always possible to learn from the best in the field, and benchmarking a program with high performers is an excellent way to do it.

Within the specialized niche of family protection, however, this is not as easy to do as in other areas. One way to do it is to network and compare notes with other directors of security and family protection managers; another is to hire a third-party provider with a proven track record of excellence in family security to perform a comparative review.

Important ongoing wins

The wins we want in sustaining successful programs are continuous and will typically be baked into the program itself. Remember, success breeds success...until it doesn't. Never get complacent!

No matter what transition is the next one for a family security program, one thing is sure: We are never better than our last detail. So, step up and never step down. Constant focus on quality deliveries should always be an objective for the entire team as they rise above self-limiting behavior to meet the ever-changing challenges of best-in-class family security.

Chapter 21:
Dealing with separation and divorce

Whether we like it or not, change is the only constant. And like every other aspect of life, the family situations of the high net worth are also subject to constant change. People meet and fall in love. They change addresses and jobs. Children are born, grow up, go away to college and start families of their own. And couples separate and get divorced; not always, by any means, but often enough for this to be an issue for security programs.

The dissolution of any marriage is a difficult transition. At best, a divorce is a disappointment; at worst, a tragedy that scars ex-spouses and family members for years. In addition to the emotional and parental challenges, there can be legal, financial, and many other practical complications, too. If the divorce involves highly prominent people whose every move is scrutinized in the media, and whose actions will be tried in the court of public opinion, then the pressure is even greater. Personal and corporate brands and income may be at stake, in addition to emotional wellbeing.

In or out?

One of the practical, on-the-ground challenges facing security teams as a result of separation or divorce is granting the ex-spouse access to a residence. Someone who may have buzzed themselves in for years may suddenly be locked out of a property that was formerly called home. If a suddenly-former principal asks to be let in, security agents must check with the still-current principal for permission to enter the property – even if the reason for the visit is to pick up children of shared custody.

This simple issue of access to a residence is emblematic of the challenges security teams face, in general, in the case of separation or divorce. If the breakup is amicable, as they often are, this will probably not create problems. If the breakup is less than friendly, security agents must pay even more attention to protocols as agreed with the current principal – as well as the feelings of both past and current principals. No matter what, security agents and managers will be required to call on all of their emotional intelligence and professionalism.

Team dynamics are always affected by a divorce

Team dynamics can change drastically when security programs must deal with divorce or separation. Perhaps, each ex-spouse continues to receive security coverage as previously, requiring additional security teams and a new security director. New residences may be added along with new family members, and teams must be scaled accordingly. Or, it may be the case that only one of the principals continues to receive coverage, and an ex-spouse may no longer benefit from any form of enhanced security.

No matter what, cooperation between existing and new security programs is key – both on the part of the principals and on the part of the security teams. A new security director hired for one ex-spouse will need to get along – without a hitch – with the existing security director for the other ex-spouse. Egos can easily get in the way of successful transitions.

Neutrality and confidentiality are a must

Divorces can precipitate an emotional maelstrom of betrayed feelings, strained loyalties, and shifting alliances. Whenever children are involved, the stakes get even higher.

Security teams are peripherally but necessarily involved and must tread carefully. Agents and managers might have some information that would be highly pertinent to one parent, who might be very persistent in trying to extract any information possible on an ex-spouse from them as well as children and household staff. Depending on their age, child principals negotiating their new family situations might become inappropriately dependent on one or more security agent(s) or resistant to security services.

Complete confidentiality and Swiss-like neutrality are the only options for security teams serving families facing the changes that divorce and separation bring in their wake. When emotions run high, security professionals must keep theirs in check. If they allow themselves to get caught up in the crossfire of shifting loyalties and hurt feelings, they will add to the family's troubles, not ameliorate them. And they will be on their way to looking for new work.

The importance of proactive planning and clear communication when dealing with divorces

That security teams must tread lightly during the transitions of a divorce does not mean they must not do anything. Security directors who take a proactive approach in engaging the principals or their representatives in order to understand the principals' priorities, and shape the contours of their security services accordingly, are much more likely to succeed in supporting the family and ensuring the professionalism of the security program.

Adjusting the security team's deliveries and roles to the realities of a post-divorce situation is essential to making the transition as smooth as possible. To do this, an open conversation with the principals early on is helpful. Relevant topics could include:

- Housing arrangements: Who lives where, who gets what? Who will manage residential security teams, systems and alarms? How will that change?

- Will both principals need protection? Who is responsible for deciding? If both spouses need protection, who will pay for what?

- Should the security team's makeup and roles change due to the breakup? Who goes where and with whom? Will security be handled by the same company or does it make sense to have two different suppliers?

- Do the children need protection? When, where and how? How should their protection be facilitated during family or public functions when both parents are present?

Of course, just what is discussed and eventually decided will depend on individual circumstances.

Part IV:

Family security is a people business – Some tips for the people who work in the field, the people that manage them, and the people that hire them

Introduction to Part IV

Talking about personality in professional contexts is not easy. For one thing, it's, err, personal, and crossing someone's emotional boundaries is always a risk. For another, none of us has trained as a psychologist, so our way of dealing with personality types isn't grounded in any kind of academic training or rigorous scientific tradition. It's more lessons learned the hard way than anything we've studied in school.

Still, we think it's fair to say that while protective security is many things, it is also a people business. Close protection is close. Traveling with a security driver puts someone else in the driver's seat. Residential security means having paid strangers around your home, dealing with your significant others, your children, your pets, and your pet peeves.

If you are new to security programs – either as a practitioner or on the client side – we hope the final section of our book will be helpful in understanding some of the traits that separate great security agents and managers from the less great.

We start with the story of Mark.

As a young, inexperienced agent, Mark hadn't yet learned an important lesson: Security agents need to be friendly, but they needn't be friends with the principal. In fact, they should never even try.

Mark learned this the hard way, and he paid the price. Fortunately, he possessed a lot of the personality traits we can include under the rubric of "the soft skills" of good protective agents, and he went on to thrive in the industry.

Chapters 22 and 23 take a look at these soft skills in two different ways. In Chapter 22 we briefly describe 10 personality traits to look for in successful protective agents. Half of these are what you could call types of "emotional intelligence" and would be helpful practically anywhere; the other half relate more specifically to careers in protective security; all are important. Chapter 23 argues that good protective agents need to be social chameleons, adapting quickly and effortlessly to the changing needs of different clients. This isn't about being fake. It's about being perceptive to other people's sensibilities and needs.

We believe Chapters 24 and 25 will have particular relevance for security directors and managers, who need to possess not only all the personality traits we discuss in the previous chapters, but find ways to develop them in others, too. Chapter 24 narrows our focus to team leads and security directors. In it, we examine some of the personal challenges that people in leadership roles typically face, the mistakes they commonly make, and make some suggestions on how to deal with them. Chapter 25 looks at the importance of creating a culture of excellence on security teams and some of the things we've discovered about this through the years.

We close our book with some thoughts on how the alpha creatures of the security world can deal successfully with the alpha creatures of the media world. Chapter 25 suggests how protection professionals can deal with paparazzi and other media, some of whom can be so aggressive and tricky that they are downright irksome. Protective agents need to keep their competitive juices and emotions in check so they themselves do not land on the front page.

The story of Mark

When Mark was still relatively new in the industry, he had a client relationship that he learned a lot from. Even though he worked with the principal for almost five years, they just didn't relate very well. For starters, the guy had all the empathy of a reptile. And then there was the fact that he was a snowflake who easily took offense. Mark was young and not very experienced. They sometimes spent hours on end together. Sometimes they'd chit chat and Mark would crack the occasional joke, trying to be funny to get on his good side, but also just to pass the time. Mark can see now, with 20-20 hindsight, that he tried too hard at making conversation and making friends. Anyway, Mark and the client once got talking about beautiful women, one of the client's favorite subjects. This guy had money, fame and power, and he used it all to his advantage. The conversation turned to the observation that beautiful women don't always have to try very hard to start or stay in a relationship if they don't want to, since so many men would be willing to do about anything just to be next to them. They were laughing, and he agreed wholeheartedly. To lighten things up even more, Mark said something like, "Yeah, but when you're an ugly guy like you or me, you have to work hard for every-thing". Dead silence. Then, "Yeah, but I'm not ugly". Oops. The guy totally missed Mark's ironic comradery and was now insulted that Mark called him ugly. Mark went into smart-ass damage control and dug himself even deeper. "Well, wouldn't it be weird if I told you that you're an attractive guy?" That didn't make things any better. The relationship never really recovered. If Mark had to do it all over again – or give advice to a younger ver-sion of himself, he'd just say, "Keep your mouth shut and do the job. You're there to provide protection and facilitate the guy's productivity, not to be his buddy. Quit trying to be Mr. Johnny on the Spot or Mr. Anything, and just do the work".

Chapter 22:
The personality traits to look for in successful protective agents

In addition to the hard skills and experience, successful family security agents possess a number of other characteristics that can be broadly described as soft skills or personality traits.

In this chapter, we outline the ten traits that set apart high-performing family protection agents from the less-than-great. Many are interrelated; all are important. When an individual agent displays most or all of these traits strongly, he or she would make a highly successful family protection agent – and would also do well in many other fields.

The first five traits are particularly significant for the special demands of the protective service industry. Because our overarching goals are to keep our principals safe, happy and productive no matter where their jobs and other interests take them, we must consistently come up with solutions to new challenges. We spend a lot of time with principals without being their friends, which requires a certain kind of person to thrive in this context.

The second five traits focus on emotional intelligence (also called EQ), which is also essential for success in family security protection. Daniel Goleman[5], who has written extensively on the matter, sums up some key concepts relative to EQ and leadership. We believe these traits apply just as well to family security agents as they do to CEOs.

1. Resourcefulness: A good family security protection agent needs a special mix of smarts and moxie. We call it resourcefulness

Family protection personnel, especially close protection agents, are often in situations that are completely new. Changes of venue, tasks, expectations, and many other aspects of the job are commonplace. Even the best standard operating procedures are tested by nonstandard situations. If there is confusion, the protection agent is the one everyone looks to make it all good again.

Resourceful protection agents make do with what they've got and always try to get the best outcome out of any situation. They're creative problem solvers, adaptive and quick to think on their feet. They ask for what they need – and aren't too shy to ask

---

[5] For more about emotional intelligence, see Goleman, Daniel, *Emotional Intelligence* (1995), (first printing) Bantam Books; see also online media.

loudly if that's what's required to get the job done. They always have a Plan B and C. And they never act as if there is anything but Plan A.

The mental habit of thinking ahead is another characteristic of a resourceful protective agents, for as Seneca pointed out several thousand years ago, "Luck is what happens when preparation meets opportunity". Good agents make their own luck – and deliver superior results – through forward thinking. Their approach resembles that of a chess player more than a checkers fan: They are used to thinking several moves ahead so that they can shape outcomes proactively rather than deal reactively with adverse situations.

2. Resilience: Life is full of stress, and bad things happen – also to good family security protection agents

Resilient protective agents aren't the ones who never get into tough situations. We all do that. They're the ones who cope with adversity and keep the mission on track no matter what. Helplessness is never an option.

Psychologically, resilient agents are able to navigate through emotional turmoil without turning into a shipwreck. They exude a calm sense of urgency whether everything is business as usual or the situation has leapt into emergency mode. They have the skills and the mindset to counterbalance negative emotions with positive ones. Even when others are succumbing to negativity and pessimism, resilient agents know how and where to dig deep to find more optimism.

3. Professional commitment: Commitment to the task of serving the principal and his or her family is an essential part of family protection

Good agents realize that the security, privacy, and productivity of the principal come first, and that the needs of the principal and his or her family supersede their own needs. They are able to put their personal preferences aside and stand by the client no matter what – before, during, and after the detail.

Successful agents also realize that this form of professional commitment has nothing to do with the interpersonal commitment that friends and lovers promise each other. Professional commitment is a one-way street. It's not reciprocal, and it's not about being the friend of the principal, his or her family, or other family office staff. It's about doing the job we are tasked to do in the most professional way possible.

4. Discretion: Agents doing close protection of the principal are, well, close to the principal

That closeness extends to all kinds of situations that never can be taught at a security school, including when the principal is conducting business, traveling, enjoying time with family and friends, dealing with other family office staff, or just getting on with his or her life. Complete confidentiality is expected in all matters.

Through it all, good family security professionals must maintain their integrity and know their place. Sometimes it's in the foreground if the principal, family, or family other estate staff want to talk; often it's in the background.

5. Service-mindedness: Family security is a service industry

It's about helping other people (notably, the paying clients who have other options) to meet their needs. It's not about the client meeting the agent's needs.

If agents are not comfortable working in a job where the needs of the client take precedence over their own, then they should start looking for other work, because 95 percent of what we do in family security is directly related to taking care of the client's requirements for protection, productivity, comfort, and overall well-being. The other 15 percent of the time is spent writing up after-action reviews and expense reports. (Yes, we've noticed that adds up to more than 100 percent. See the notes on work-life balance below.)

While protective agents might sometimes stay at five-star hotels and eat at three-star Michelin restaurants, they are also the ones who clean up before the principal arrives and make sure there's plenty of the principal's and his or her family's favorite water in the car. They may have even washed the car between bites of a plastic sandwich.

Some people get the service mentality; others don't. It's not so much about being servile as it is taking ownership of the job and consistently adapting to the client's needs.

Successful family security agents do their jobs, and they help others in the family ecosystem to do theirs, too. Because they are service minded, they know that if they make the principal's estate manager, nanny, or others look good, they too will look good – and the principal's family will be more likely to be safe, happy and productive.

6. Self-awareness: Family protection professionals must know their strengths as well as their weaknesses

In addition to being clear on their own goals and motivation, they must be able to recognize how their own moods and emotions impact others.

People with a well-developed sense of self-awareness exude self-confidence. They're also able to laugh at themselves and feel no need to over- or underestimate their own abilities.

7. Self-regulation: Family protection agents need a high degree of self-regulation in order to stay open to change and deal with new or ambiguous situations

Good self-regulation helps them choose their words carefully – and gives them the option of thinking before reacting.

Great family protection agents also master another, very particular form of self-regulation. They are able to remain vigilant for hours on end when absolutely nothing is happening. Moment-by-moment situational awareness is key to protection.

8. Social skills: Family protection agents must be able to work with people and build relationships in order to make things happen

The best agents are born networkers who lay the groundwork of solid connections everywhere from the front gate to the kitchen. They find common ground where others find barriers, and they build good rapport wherever they can.

They're also excellent communicators who get their message across and have the persuasiveness to get their way more often than not. They can read a principal, the family, or family estate staff, and any situation; they know when it's time to fade into the background, and when it's time to engage in conversation; and they understand the difference between assertiveness and aggression.

9. Empathy: Empathy starts with being aware of other people' s feelings, then considering these feelings when we take action

For the family security agent, these "other people" include not only the principal, but everyone else in his or her orbit – also other folks working for the family in any capacity.

Empathic family security agents thrive in both home and international settings. They pick up on verbal and nonverbal cues that express an individual personality, a family's culture, or an entire nation's way of relating and doing business. They recognize the needs of others. And they act accordingly.

But the empathy of good family security protection agents is controlled, not unrestrained. Controlled empathy enables the successful family protection agent to temper warm compassion with cool calculation. Good agents don't drop standard operating procedures to please the principal, the family, or the estate staff. But as we saw above in Tom's story, neither do they beat others up with stiff adherence to protocol in every imaginable situation. They recognize how people are feeling and acknowledge those feelings through their actions without losing sight of the overall program objectives.

10. Self-motivation: It is variously called drive, initiative, perseverance and being proactive

Highly motivated protection agents don't do the job for the money or the recognition. They achieve for the sake of achievement.

A self-motivated family security agent is a good family security agent. He or she maintains an optimistic outlook even when the chips are down. A high degree of motivation means the performance bar is always on the way up, and continual improvement is a way of life.

Chapter 23:
Good family protective agents and managers need to be social chameleons

A good security director and family protection agent is a social chameleon.

Chameleons have the amazing ability to change the color of their skin according to their surroundings or mood. They can blend into the background to escape danger. They can stand out to attract a mate. And they perform their chromatic magic dynamically, instantly switching colors as the situation demands.

Security directors & family protection agents would do well to learn from the chameleon's adaptive strategy. They too must both blend in and stand out. And they must do it quickly and seamlessly with every new assignment.

For most of us in this business, the standing out part is not hard. Indeed, the stereotypical image of burly bodyguards in black is all about making a show of protection. But it's not something most of our principals are too keen on. In fact, one of the most overlooked competences in family protection is the ability to fit in.

There is no one way of doing things

Family protection agents need to communicate and interact with principals who are as different as night and day. As agents move with them through their business and often private lives, they must relate to all kinds of people and cultures. In order to be truly skilled in family protection, agents must be able to blend in with any principal in any environment and adjust to any social situation. In short, they need to be what we could call a "social chameleon".

Many who work in executive protection – even those with years of experience – believe there is only one way of interacting with the principal, and that this one way is the best way. This belief is often based on a career that has exposed them to one tech CEO, one government agency, or one celebrity.

As people who have been fortunate enough to work with a wide variety of principals in very different contexts, we can knowledgeably say that this is not the case.

While protecting a Grammy-winning hip hop artist, we've dressed and spoken completely differently than we did when working with the Hollywood fashion icon. This was also different from working with the relaxed Silicon Valley billionaire, who provided yet another experience than working with the straight-laced corporate executive who was rarely seen in anything but a three-piece suit.

It might seem silly, but when one of our agents replaced the Brooks Brothers look with some sneakers, jeans and a hat, our musician client just felt more comfortable. Without really thinking about it, the agent's speech patterns changed from "Yes Sir, I'll get on that right away, Mr. Principal", to a more informal tone that the client shared with other people in his inner circle. Of course, this type of friendly interaction would have been unacceptable with any of our suit-wearing corporate clients.

Understanding the principal's personal preferences: It's more than clothes

But this is about more than appearance and language. It's also about understanding the principal's personal preferences in all kinds of other ways.

For example, we worked for a long time for one of the most popular – and controversial – hosts on television. Before our first detail, we made it a point to do some prep work to find out what the guy was into and discovered that he was a huge fan of baseball, in general, and of the New York Mets, in particular. Now some might call us un-American because we're not really baseball fans at all, but because we knew our principal was a major-league fanatic, we did our research. The night before we met him, we read up on the Mets on some online sports columns. It paid off the very next morning.

While driving him to work (knowing beforehand that he likes to pass the time by talking about sports), he asked one of us if we knew the score from last night's game between the Twins and the Mets. Surprisingly, one of us did. We were able to chat with him back and forth in great detail about a sport that we couldn't previously name three players in. Talking over game stats made the principal comfortable and distracted him from the numerous threats he had received regarding an event he was putting on.

One thing we've learned: Making the effort to connect socially in an appropriate way can be very helpful. Another thing we've learned is that that doesn't make you a friend.

No two clients are alike. So, make it part of SOPs to treat them all in nonstandard ways

We've heard the following way too often: "I learned in ___X___ that the correct way to interact with a principal is ___Y___".

Now, everyone fills in the blanks in his or her own way, depending on where they got their fixed ideas about how to do protective security. X could be an executive protection school, the military, the government, a police department, or even the guy's last detail. But while everyone's take on the question is a little different, they are all convinced that their answer is the most correct.

To succeed in family security, you have to be smart, analytical, and adaptable in your approach. Every time. Why should ours be the first profession that rewards people for trying to fit square pegs into round holes?

Every principal is different. What's more, their needs evolve and change. If you're used to working with principals in corporate settings and you carry that way of doing things over into work in the sports or entertainment industry or with families, it won't work. Ditto on the vice versa. Old-school corporate culture is one thing. Silicon Valley corporate culture is another.

Family ecosystems are another. The worlds of sports and entertainment and the family are different from one another.

Even in Hollywood, where looks and images are worth millions, we've seen agents who couldn't be bothered to adapt themselves to their principal. Or maybe, they just didn't understand how important it is to do so.

We once served a principal who was very big in the fashion world and seen as one of the most glamorous and best-dressed people in a city that has more than its fair share of good looking folks. One of the agents on the team was physically capable, smart and intelligent, but was really lacking in social (and sartorial) savvy. He didn't get that since he was working with a fashion icon, he needed to dress the part and buy some decent designer jeans, shirts, shoes, etc. Instead, he chose to be an individual and dress for work the way he dressed for everything else: in some out-of-date baggy Levi's jeans, a faded Docker shirt, and tactical sunglasses. We've got nothing against Walmart, but if you're working for a Hollywood A-list celeb who's consistently shortlisted for the title of the best-dressed woman on the planet, you might want to find some of your clothes elsewhere.

Guess what? He ended up embarrassing the principal, who saw him as an extension of herself and her brand image, so he was let go. Seems harsh? Not really. That's the world we live in, and this guy just didn't get it. The tough part is that's also the way he had chosen to dress for his previous principal, a famous rock musician, and it was completely acceptable in that case. But each principal is different, and he couldn't or wouldn't adapt.

When "up close and personal" is part of the job description, agents need a good sense of discretion

Keeping the principal and his or her family office and family comfortable really can be challenging at times. Especially if on a detail that keeps an agent right there at practically every waking hour of their day. And yes, this can include the most intimate times with their family, trips to the restroom, and a visit to the White House to meet the president.

It might seem glamorous, but being someone that is famous, always under public scrutiny, the constant target of direct and indirect threats, and surrounded by security, really take its toll.

Some agents think themselves smart and charming. If agents spend enough time around anyone, they are going to annoy them. That's why the best family security agents become masters of neutrality and assiduously avoid displays of annoying personality traits. Of course, you can't just erase a personality out of the equation, but there are few tricks of the trade that can really make an agent's presence more neutral.

One way that we use frequently is to avoid standing in direct eye contact with the principal while he or she is meeting with or talking with anyone. Maintaining eyeball-to-eyeball line of sight with someone in protection is going to end up smothering them. The solution is simple: We tell agents to stand to the side or behind them – give them some agent-neutral space, a break from seeing a pretty face, but still be in a tactical position to respond if needed.

Silence is another powerful tool. We train our agents to learn to use it. We've been on five-hour road trips while sitting next to the principal and not a word was spoken between us. Absolute silence: no music, no small talk, no nothing for five long hours.

As we saw in the story of "Mark", less experienced agents can start to feel awkward and try to fill the dead space with idle chatter. But when a principal and/or the family are famous and everyone in the world outside the car wants to ask questions about being famous or tell you stories about theirs, conversation can be the most aggravating thing in the world. A break in the talk stream can feel like a luxurious holiday. Silence is a good thing. When it comes up, leave it alone.

Dig in, read up

Being a good social chameleon doesn't mean acting like an illiterate reptile. When our agents travel with a principal and or the family to other countries, it pays to do a little research before getting into the plane.

We've collectively been to almost every country in the world on protection details, and every time we travel somewhere we haven't been before, we try to learn something about the cultural behavior of the people we'll be visiting. We ask our agents to read the many excellent books on practically every culture on Earth, or just to Google "social taboos, country X" or "what not to do as a foreigner traveling to country X". It won't make them experts, but it can help them not to look like idiots.

For example, before you go to Japan, learn that it's rude to point, accept things with one hand, lean back in your chair, and show the bottom of your feet while sitting. Our agents don't need to become an expert in Zen tea ceremonies. But they do need to understand that there's a little ritual around exchanging business cards. There have been plenty of situations where we could clue in the principal on proper cultural etiquette, which makes them look well-informed and makes us look impressive. After all, we're not only there to make sure they are protected, we're there to prevent them from any sort of embarrassment.

When our agents need to communicate and don't have the luxury of a shared tongue, body language is invaluable. An experienced protection professional can negotiate transportation, ask for help, buy food in a market, and get directions from a stranger through hand motions alone. Remember, too that body language can get lost in translation. A typical gesture from your country might mean something completely different in other parts of the world. It's wise for Americans to know that the V for victory, or peace sign, means "up yours" in the UK and Australia, that showing your palms in Greece is insulting, and that giving the thumbs up in Thailand is a sign of condemnation.

We tell our agents, "Go ahead and act natural"

Bringing all of this together to adapt to a family ecosystem isn't a simple thing to do. One of the toughest parts for someone new to the business is coming off as genuine rather than someone playing a bit part in a high school play. The tricky part here is that being a social chameleon only works when agents are truly genuine. This can't be an act, it needs to be real.

Every person walking the earth has different sides that come to the fore in different situations. This isn't about being a fake. It's about being perceptive to other people's sensibilities and needs.

We tell agents to think of some examples from their own lives. The way they talk to a grandmother at her dining table is probably very different from the way they talk to their buddies in the locker room. Agents must not act in exactly the same way around co-workers as they do with their wives, brothers, best friends, or worst enemies. Agents adapt to varying social situations for their own good and for the good of the folks who are being protected.

The same holds true for how agents choose to communicate with a principal and/or the family. The relationship is unique, and at the end of the day that's perfectly all right. Close protection is being true to one's self and perceiving any special social circumstances.

Bruce Lee said it best: "You must be shapeless, formless, like water. When you pour water in a cup, it becomes the cup. When you pour water in a bottle, it becomes the bottle. When you pour water in a teapot, it becomes the teapot. Water can drip, and it can crash. Become like water, my friend."

It's not about the agent

One of our tenets is that when we protect principals and their families as they move through their daily lives, there's no room for our personal opinions, beliefs, philosophies, or ideas. It's not about our needs, it's about the principals and the family culture.

Of course, we are our own people, but our personal opinions aren't our principal's business or the family's business. Our philosophy and personalities while providing a service must match the principal's and the family's sensibilities and needs. We must adapt to the changes a principal and the family make.

The same holds true for communication style. Agents must adapt to the principal's, the estate staff's, and the family's communication styles to eliminate unneeded friction and confusion. This is easier said than done: Agent social skills and adaptability vary and some of them seem more or less baked into their personalities. They are tough to learn if they don't come naturally. And while we think everyone can learn and improve at least to some extent, some people just don't have the psychological makeup that will help them become happy campers as effective social chameleons.

Don't fly too close to the sun

One of our favorite stories in Greek mythology is the tale of Daedalus and Icarus.

The father-son duo was imprisoned by a king, but Daedalus, a brilliant engineer, found a way to escape: He fashioned wings from feathers and wax so that he and his son could fly over the prison walls to freedom. Although Daedalus warned his son not to fly too high, Icarus was tempted and flew high in the sky and much too close to the sun. In so doing, the wax in his wings melted, and he fell into the sea and died.

The old adage, "Don't fly too close to the sun, or you'll get burned" is also true for protection professionals. In our world, the principal can be seen as the sun: Although many are powerful and charming, it can in fact be dangerous to get too close. If flying too high and getting chummy with the principal, the staff, or family members, an agent may become overconfident and start taking risks, ignoring warning signs because being close to the sun is glorious and thrilling. This all happens because the real interests of the principals were not understood.

Agents who have long and successful careers in our field, working close to the sun (our principals, and their families, and staff) every day, have learned how to insulate themselves from personal relationships with the principal. These agents don't need to be friends with the family. They strive to be a part of the small percentage of people in the family's life that doesn't want something from them.

Successful security professionals do not ask for favors. They do not ask for business advice. They do not ask for friendship.

They do understand that most people around a celebrity, billionaire, or any other prominent public figure have their hands out and want a piece of that money, notoriety, or fame.

Chapter 24:
The common mistakes security directors need to stop making

Everybody slips up sometimes. We're only human after all. And as Hall of Fame basketball coach John Wooden pointed out, "If you're not making mistakes, then you're not doing anything." The wisdom of this statement is, of course, not to encourage inaction to avoid mistakes, but to learn from them.

So, in the spirit of helping everyone working in family security, here's a list of mistakes we have seen security directors make too many times – and can learn from.

1. They make things personal

Family security is a service industry. It's always about the principal and his or her family. It's about providing principals and the entire family ecosystem with knowhow, activities, and circumstances that keep them safe, happy and productive. It's not about the protective agents.

Life happens – also on protection details. Good security managers keep personal issues out of the job. They do a lot of listening, not talking. The friendly "How are you?" gets answered with a "Good, and you?"

2. They try to recreate where they came from rather than adapt to where they are

It's natural to use experience from the past to deal with the present, but this can also lead to problems. Security managers with backgrounds in the military, law enforcement, or even just another family need to adapt their practices to the context they are in, not try to change that context to be more like where they came from.

This goes for language, too. Be sure to communicate in a way that others in the ecosystem can understand – without having to learn all of the abbreviations and other jargon that you learned along the way.

3. They forget they're running a service *business*

This is also a business, and team leaders and security managers need to think like business people, in addition to thinking about the operational aspects of security. We're not saying that an MBA is needed, but here are a few basics:

- *Sales and marketing:* Must be ready to describe the features of what the team does, and how these features of our security programs create tangible benefits for the client in terms of both security and productivity. Know what additional services the company is capable of providing and how to get these on the radar in an appropriate way, if relevant. And make sure everyone on the team can do the same thing.

- *Finance:* Know the numbers. Understand the budgets and actual figures and how these are used both within one's own company and by the client. Keep a sharp eye on program expenses and how they track against budgets. Think like a CFO, even when the program is just part of the bigger picture. It always pays off.

- *HR:* Attract, retain, and develop talent, and there is a lot of competition for the best talent. How to do this in both the short and long term? Good HR people do more than get all of the admin things right, e.g., salaries, benefits, and compliance issues. They also think strategically to make sure their teams are ready for what's coming around the next curve.

4. They don't show respect for estate personnel and others in the family ecosystem

This problem arises when family security managers and agent think *their* work is more significant than the work of the principal's executive assistant, estate manager, nanny, chef, house cleaner, or other staff. As we saw with Mark, if the manager is on good footing with the principal but not with everyone else, this manager won't last for long.

5. They and their agents don't blend in with the principal's and family's lifestyle

If agents come off as too militaristic, the clients may feel like prisoners in their own homes. If agents are like Robocops around the spouse and children, these family members are unlikely to feel comfortable even though they might be safe. And even agent Mr. Personality might need to take a chill pill, because his perky greetings and chattiness may start getting on people's nerves. Agents should blend in, so the client never has to think "Who is this guy?!"

6. They forget to check their egos at the door

We've seen it happen more than once. A guy who is a capable operator rises through the ranks to assume some management responsibility. He's very aware of his role and perceived power, and he wields it to his own advantage without worrying about how that impacts other members of the protective team. Eventually, the principal or family office will get the whole story and the manager's job will be over.

7. They play favorites or allow the principal to do so

This is another pitfall that too many security managers dive right into. It's understandable because it's human nature to want to be liked. And it's yet another a good example of "seemed like a good idea at the time".

Cultivating a culture of favoritism damages team readiness. It's unhealthy for the wellbeing of the protection program, the principal and the family. And it's not a sustainable foundation for anything. The simple fact of the matter is that favorites come and go. With our history of developing and managing executive protection and family security programs, we see people fall into the favorites trap all too often.

Favoritism starts out innocently enough and often with the best intentions. The principal really likes Tim, and Tim has to do everything. That's a win-win for a short while, but it soon turns counterproductive.

The detail rapidly becomes a logistical nightmare. Tim will burn out – he's too close to the principal and working too many hours. The rest of the team will suffer – they come off like second-class citizens. The solution is to build everyone up to Tim's level, not to turn Tim into a fast-flaming fave.

The risks of favoritism need to be explained to both the team, the principals, estate staff, and family members to ensure everyone understands the problems and the solution. It shouldn't matter who is providing coverage because the services should be delivered in the same way. Rotation of team members is an important part of that, and managers should be prepared to discuss this with everyone involved – including principals.

Agent travel with the family is a fertile breeding ground for favoritism. Managers must continue to rotate agent duties to prevent this.

8. They let their inner control freak run wild, and say "either/or" rather than "and"

We're all for being sticklers when it comes to security and following the standard operating procedures (SOPs) designed to safeguard principals and family members. But even the best of plans sometimes are broadsided by the principal and/or the family. And all for good reason, i.e., whatever the principal and or the family say, it is.

Or doesn't say. You see, it's the principal's business and family plans that matter, not the security manager's or agent's. Business opportunities arise suddenly; family travel plans change suddenly; teenagers do stupid things. It doesn't matter. Protective teams are on the clock of family security, not their own. And they need to make things work according to the family's priorities, not their own.

Family priorities trump schedules, plans, and procedures every time. This can be tough for the pack of alpha males and females who often end up in our industry. We're used to being in control, and we plan carefully. But if a manager can't control it, he or she must just embrace it: This creates less stress for all involved.

9. They try to take financial advantage of their positions

Working with C-suite executives, celebrities, and other high net worth clients means moving about in some very different environments than most of us are used to. An agent may be bunking at the Motel 6 one day and staying at the Four Seasons the next. People who one day look at the cost per pound when shopping for hot dogs at the supermarket might looking at a menu that doesn't have prices on it the next day.

Even though the client is wealthy, money does matter – both in terms of how others will view the judgement and integrity of managers and agents – and to the family security program success. There's always a budget for everything. Managers who go far in this industry respect the client's wallet and work to save their money – and make sure that everyone on the team does the same thing.

10. They fog up information transparency – a.k.a. lying or being selectively honest

It's true now and it's been true for thousands of years: Information is power, and asymmetrical access to information can give a competitive advantage or disadvantage. That's great if you're fighting a war, but it's really not good if security managers allow this to happen.

We're not saying that everyone needs to know everything. But security managers who deliberately resist sharing information, reduce information transparency, or spread false information are on their way to career suicide.

Some inexperienced managers might have the erroneous belief that hoarding information will further their interests. They're making a fundamental mistake. They haven't understood that what's good for the team is good for the principal, the family, or for themselves. We've seen managers try to keep estate staff in the dark to make them look incompetent. We've heard of managers who say the principal's spouse prefers this or that driver – even when that wasn't the case – to play favorites or gain personal advantage.

People like this are worse than dishonest. If they're willing to hijack parts of the program for their own reasons, what else are they willing to do? Their reasons are never good and manipulating the healthy flow of useful information always hits them in the back of the head like a boomerang.

11. They don't create the right balance between tactical discipline and friendly service

Good family security agents juggle multiple roles seamlessly and imperceptibly. They are the tactical "tough guy" when needed. They are the friendly concierge if that's what's called for. They know not to overplay either hand. And they know when to switch immediately.

Good security directors know there are often multiple ways to accomplish the same objective. They balance situational and social awareness with security SOPs to find the ideal path, striking a middle way between the many possible extremes.

They also know that all their agents need to be service-minded, but not excessively friendly in all circumstances. Protection agents should always facilitate the principal's or the family's smooth flow through the day and night but should be willing to stand up and disrupt the good vibes if that means maintaining security. They must never be afraid to tell the principal if his or her decision increases risk.

We've emphasized the importance of adapting security to the principal's preferences over and over again. But this doesn't mean acquiescing blindly to any and every whim the principal might express. It is our job to mitigate risk. If the principal's actions and decisions increase risk, it is our job to point this out, not simply to say "yes". No one wants a "yes man" for a security director – especially not the principal.

Maybe, the principal wants security, but is he or she unwilling to accept any security measures? This makes it almost impossible for the security director to succeed. Or perhaps principals want to define their own security configurations on what they've seen provided for friends, not on the security director's recommendations? By simply saying yes, the security director would put the convenience of making the principal happy above the imperative of keeping him or her safe.

Of course, balancing the principal's personal preferences with best-practice security procedures is never a cut-and-dried affair. Compromises are needed here as in so many other aspects of life. But the security director who always errs on the side of pleasing the principal – at the expense of protecting him or her – is running a program that will rarely end well.

Let's learn from mission mistakes

The good thing about mistakes is that they're learning opportunities: They help us to discover better ways of doing things. It's only when security managers and agents continue to make the same mistakes over and over that people start doubting the protection detail. Similarly, not learning from others' mistakes is rarely an indication of a sharp mind.

We admit that we've learned some of them the hard way – by putting our own hands in the flames, so to speak. Other lessons came easier, by observing colleagues and staff get burned themselves. But they're all things we as protection professionals strive to be aware of and get better at.

Chapter 25:
How security leaders ensure that program excellence starts with every team member

Excellence is the only acceptable standard for family protection programs. Who wants second best?

Developing and maintaining excellent family protection programs requires that security directors establish a culture of trust. Everyone on the team, from the guys pulling the midnight shift at the gate to the team lead responsible for an estate's overall security should understand, live, and breathe the foundations of this trust: integrity, personal responsibility, and mutual respect.

- ***Integrity*** in communications and effective problem solving demand that people be honest and forthcoming – even when it's difficult – and always pursue a constructive outcome.

- ***Personal responsibility*** holds everyone accountable for his or her actions – and inaction. Mistakes will be made. When team members own up to their mistakes, it makes diagnosing and fixing problems easier. When they *own* their mistakes, it indicates that there is trust.

- ***Mutual respect*** secures a safe working environment for people to perform confidently, knowing that mistakes are opportunities to improve the program, rather than opportunities to make others look bad.

Even when everyone on the team is working hard to make the program excel, things do not always go as planned. That people make mistakes is a fact-of-life. When this happens, team communication that respects the foundations of trust must always be constructive and for the purpose of professional development. We want to focus on solutions, not on blame, as we get to the root causes of an issue and fix it.

Excellent family security programs are both data- and feedback-driven

As we discussed in Chapter 13, it is critical that security managers collect and analyze data that is relevant to team performance and establish solid KPIs to keep ongoing track of how the team is living up to agreed objectives. Regardless of whether or not the principal or the stakeholder in the ecosystem is interested in the metrics, a team leader should always collect and monitor them. Understanding the data around a program also supports branding and storytelling efforts that build the team's reputation and value proposition.

But feedback from the principal and team are also critical to success. Every family security team member has a responsibility to voice concerns, objections, and opinions about all facets of our operations. To ensure that a culture of trust is maintained on the team, and that the team is forthcoming with the feedback that is so important to keep the program on track, we offer the following lessons learned (in no particular order):

- The keys to long-term success are quality engagement with clients and employees, quality control, and procedural and technological innovation.

- Criticism should be voiced in a constructive manner – with development in mind.

- Once a problem is identified, then offer ideas for a solution.

- Problems are opportunities to be excellent – someone doesn't always need to be at fault.

- We succeed and fail together as a team and as a program.

- We must be committed to each other's professional development.

- Every team member is equal, and all positions are essential to success.

- Real-time feedback needs to be given to the agents on the team: The principal likes it when you do this, doesn't like it when you do that. If the principal isn't happy with this, please fix it, etc.

- Team leads need monthly syncs with security directors and representatives of the principal.

- Inclusion is huge: If they're just "gate guards", programs will suffer.

- Find each team member's passion and play to their strengths. Some folks are good at organizing and like cool gadgets, so put them in charge of medical; others are good on the computer, so have them create and maintain advance manuals, etc.

- To give and get feedback, employees need daily engagement whether through reports, calls, emails, messenger apps, etc.

Remember that good employees are not in it solely for the money

We all thrive best when we are learning and growing, so team leads and managers need to consider and implement ways to facilitate such personal growth:

- Training is a huge motivator: It sharpens skills and prevents complacency.

- Consider the personal development of employees as an investment that is critical in establishing a healthy workplace culture.

- Schedule roundtable discussions with the team to discuss career growth and encourage open dialog about professional growth.

- Encourage personal days for all team members.

- Maintaining a healthy work-life balance can be difficult in our industry, as the principal's needs always come first. Managers can help by:

  o Flexible scheduling, e.g., working several days in a row and then having several days off to spend with families; mixing longer and shorter shifts, etc.

  o Offer paid time off for family issues, child care, volunteering, and opportunities to explore interests and passions

- Create mentorship opportunities that expose mentees to experienced professionals and different aspects of the protective security business.

- Set up regular, one-to-one meetings and be sure to listen when you ask employees open-ended questions about their work and solicit feedback on how to more effectively support them in their work.

- Recognize success and celebrate wins with the team.

The importance of instilling a shared sense of purpose

If you're a team lead or a manager, are you prepared to answer if the principal asks, "Do you think I need security?" Is everyone on your team prepared? Would they all answer in the same way?

Let's hope so. Because if everyone on the team provides a consistent response to this query, that's a strong indication of a shared sense of purpose.

Program excellence depends on each and every team member understanding the purpose of the security program and how their role contributes to fulfilling that purpose. The safety of the principals is paramount, of course, and that's why we develop standard operating procedures to mitigate the risks associated with persons of interest, unwanted approaches in public spaces, traveling by car, and all the rest. But the purpose of what we do goes beyond security to include productivity.

When a security driver is behind the wheel during the principal's commute, that enables the principal to do something more productive than navigate traffic during rush hour. When a CEO's productivity goes up, for example, this allows more people in the company to boost their productivity, too – and can make the company more competitive. When every team member, from security drivers to residential agents to the agents that travel with the principal all understand how what they do supports the double-edged purpose of safety and productivity, then we are well on our way to program excellence.

Chapter 26:
How protection professionals can deal with paparazzi and other media

When working with high profile or high net worth clients, executive protection professionals must accept that the media simply come with the territory. A clear understanding of how the media operate to access the principal is key to ensuring the principal's well-being and privacy.

To treat everyone involved with the press the same fails to account for how various media outlets work, what their aims are, which methods they're willing to employ, and their agendas. An accredited reporter from a mainstream outlet requesting an interview with the principal through official channels is one thing. Paparazzi doing all they can to bypass security and snap a shot – no matter how this affects the client's image or safety – is another.

Before we dig into some ideas on planning, protocols, and procedures, let's be sure to differentiate how we think about the media, which can be split into at least five categories.

1. The mainstream media

This includes New York Times, Washington Post, the BBC, CNN, and many others that are generally large, influential, and active worldwide. While they do have their own tricks of the trade to get information on or from the principal, we can generally expect their approach to be above board – and above planting a bug.

2. "Partisan" or "fringe" media outlets

These media outlets are also driven by their need for information about the principal. However, their editorial slant is more obvious and tends to represent certain views rather than report information neutrally. Sometimes the views fringe journalists espouse match those of the principal, and the exposure might be beneficial to the principal's image. Other times, not. Since partisan agendas can result in fabricated rumors about the principal that can be more impactful than facts, their readership should not be underestimated.

3. Gossip media

They rely on paparazzi pictures, rumor mongering, and clickable headlines to sustain their business. Here, accuracy and honorable journalistic standards matter little: These writers and photographers tend to be oriented toward revenue, page views, and clicks rather than any Pulitzer Prize aspirations. We can consequently expect them to intrude on a client's privacy by any means necessary – from greasing palms, to planting bugs, and shooting long-range pictures in any way possible.

4. Freelance or independent media

This group includes bloggers and journalists who are not affiliated with any of the aforementioned groups but operate independently and then sell the information to them. Some may resort to shady or dangerous tactics. Whether their aim is money or revealing information they consider valuable or important, they can be considered somewhat "rogue" elements who may break accepted standards to get what they want.

5. Anyone with a smartphone, which means just about everyone

Let's not forget that we're living in an extremely connected world in which everyone is a journalist – or can become one very quickly. Practically all media, from the most mainstream to the furthest fringe, have open-door policies that make it simple to submit stories and pictures in the form of anonymous tips via encrypted apps such as WhatsApp and Signal. And as we've pointed out in our first book, *Corporate Executive Protection: An Introduction for Corporations and Security Professionals,* by Christian West and Brian Jantzen, apps like Instagram, Facebook and Twitter make it even simpler for millions of people to snap a shot that can go viral in minutes.

While these categories are helpful, they are by no means absolute. To assume that all members of the mainstream media will always operate "cleanly" or that paparazzi will always use "dirty" tricks is wrong. Letting one's guard down around certain reporters or being needlessly defensive or aggressive with others may lead to unintended and problematic consequences.

Reputable media sources may have some less-reputable staff. Some independent journalists have political or personal axes to grind, others don't. Even a positive, approved interview with a major newspaper may be picked up by other outlets who put their own spin on the information. Remember that information does not exist in a vacuum and that anything (anything!) can go viral in moments. A single embarrassing picture may be re-blogged or shared on Twitter thousands of times. In fact, information may first pop up on social media *before* being acquired and spread by "proper" media outlets.

They say that good news travels fast. Well, so does bad news. Our point is that information *spreads* – sometimes very quickly. While it is impossible to control how far and the manner in which it will do so, security professionals should focus on making sure that no information leaks, and that whatever does leak will be okay with the client. We do this by thinking through our interactions with the media ahead of time and by being prepared to mitigate foreseeable risks.

Preparations, protocols, and procedures for dealing with the media

Be prepared: When the day begins, protection professionals, the principal, and everyone else in his or her entourage should have a clear idea of what to expect in terms of media encounters. Based on these expectations, we then need to make plans to deal with possible upcoming interactions, both the expected and the unexpected, and what to do whether things go well or not. Advances should always include thinking about where it is likely to run into the media, where pictures might be taken from, and how the media might attempt to move past security measures.

Know your principal and the particular risks he or she may face: A high-profile client who regularly engages with the media, or even thrives in a symbiotic relationship with the media, will in all likelihood be given a lot more attention than those known to maintain their privacy. However, the latter may also be confronted with more dedicated scoop-hunters who are desperate to glean any bit of info about the principal. If the principal is a celebrity, do they have an album or movie coming out, or is it a "quiet" period? Buzz may vary depending on the current career status. Those protecting female clients need to think about upskirt or cleavage shots taken by the *that* kind of photographer. Is the principal known to be aggressive towards the press? If so, protective agents will have to be prepared to protect them from themselves, too.

Know which media you're dealing with: Who is likely to go after the principal? How many? How do they generally operate? What is their outlet's reputation? Are they known for going to extreme lengths to get what they want? What locations have they used in the past and may use again? What resources are at their disposal? Can they use drones, helicopters, hacking? How many vehicles do they have? Have they chatted with the neighbors or the staff? We've mentioned that the media *generally* don't have a personal grudge, but sometimes they do. If so, special precautions should be taken. We can't know everything, but we can make sure that the knowable becomes part of our preparations.

Understand and manage the media: The media are what they are. To try and ignore them is to disregard the way society works and the profession's goals. Whether the principal wants to engage with the media or not, the media will be there. The majority of them don't have a personal grudge towards the client or towards protective staff. They do their job; we do ours. It is completely possible to leverage media presence into something positive. We can't make the media disappear, but we can sometimes help shape the narrative by scripting how and when an encounter will take place. When relevant and appropriate, protective professionals should work with client PR teams to select safe locations where the media can snap shots and engage with the principal. In so doing, we reduce the likelihood of an unwanted intrusion earlier or later that day; we give the reporters what they want (within reason); we help boost the client's image; and we remain in control the whole time.

Leverage local resources: Depending on the jurisdiction, law enforcement officers are generally quite good at enforcing private property rules and making sure unwanted reporters don't wander around places they shouldn't be. Security staff should be aware of the local laws wherever they are and be ready to use them to their advantage. Other security officers (such as hotel or venue security staff) who aren't necessarily part of the protective team or operation should be relied on, too. There is no reason to needlessly share information with them about the principal, but good cooperation with them can provide a broader perspective of the situation. The same is true of the principal's own team, from PR to management. We all rely on information. We should have as much as we can to do our job and provide others with enough to do theirs.

Be discrete: Since the media feed on information, security professionals must carefully manage and safeguard whatever information they might have about the principal. Never use the principal's name when booking a hotel, restaurant, or any other place that requires a reservation. Keep a tight lid on the principal's schedule, not saying a word about anything to anyone unless pre-approved. Shred documents. Keep an eye on social media. Contacting others about our principals' movements should be done without sacrificing their privacy. Consider using decoys if the principal's next location has been staked out by reporters – even a few seconds can be enough to make a safe exit.

Stay composed and keep your eye on the big picture: We've all seen those videos of security pros being way too rough with paparazzi and journalists in high-stress situations. While protective assertiveness is always warranted, keep in mind that getting physical in any way is an option of last resort, not a means of dissuasion or intimidation. Protective staff should not engage in needless banter, trash talk, or raise their voices. Their every word is potential fodder for headlines later that day. We needn't be the lion swatting at the fly: Let insults fly by unanswered and remember that what we do reflects on the client. TMZ would have no qualms about running a piece that discusses how a celebrity's security staff misbehaved. The principal's name and reputation are inherently attached to how we carry ourselves. After all, they hired *us* and will be seen with *us*. We must consider ourselves another potential way for journalists to get to the principal and act accordingly.

OK, we've just dedicated a whole chapter to paparazzi and other media. Of course, this *is* important, but it's even more important not to lose sight of the larger protective picture. Some paparazzi are so aggressive and tricky that they are downright irksome. This can get one's competitive juices flowing to the point where focus on one (extremely pesky) potential threat eclipses our awareness of other even greater threats. Let's remember that it's our job to assess the entirety of potential threats as objectively, comprehensively, and constantly as we can. Letting our emotions run away with us does no good for anyone.

Appendix:
Case studies

Rapid growth in wealth and prominence demands rapid protective response – and a personal security program that grows with evolving needs

When an entrepreneur taps a gold vein in the burgeoning digital economy, valuations can skyrocket overnight – as can personal wealth and public prominence. And along with increased prominence can come higher threat levels.

AS Solution works with many highly successful founders who have had to ramp up personal security measures from one day to the next and build protection programs that quickly evolve with changing needs.

279

The challenge: Sudden wealth leads to greatly increased prominence, new vulnerabilities, and the need to mitigate risk

The principal, the young founder of a young startup, suddenly found himself in the news as his company's valuations rose astronomically. Like most other people in his situation, personal security was the furthest thing from his mind until unwanted incidents began to pile up and his board started talking about the need for protection.

With few employees, the company had neither a security department nor any experience with executive protection. So, they turned to AS Solution to learn more about their options and make sure the principal was not taking unnecessary risks.

The solution: Quick reaction to manage the most vulnerable situations – and a flexible protection strategy to meet evolving needs

The founder traveled frequently and was headed for a city that even non-experts knew was a high-risk destination. Could AS Solution provide protection for this trip?

We quickly arranged for a security driver and an executive protection agent that could get the principal around the city in question discreetly, efficiently, and, of course, safely. Things went well.

This resulted in more secure travel support for more trips as well as event security. Discussions about deeper involvement ensued, leading to the creation of a personal protection strategy based on an analysis of pertinent risks, threats, and vulnerabilities – as well as the company's young culture and the principal's personal preferences.

The result: An iterative approach that grew to comprise comprehensive risk mitigation measures

Over the course of less than a year, the program grew alongside the principal's mounting prominence and the company's increased awareness of evolving threat levels. We progressed in small, iterative steps in order to learn as we went along, communicate with the company, and to make sure that all services were tailored to the client's preferences.

A program that began with one-off secure travel support for high-risk destinations now includes an embedded EP manager, EP and residential agents, and an intelligence analyst. Furthermore, we continue to support the principal and other executives in the company on their frequent travels domestically and abroad, typically three out of every four weeks.

A rising star experiences rising risks

Being a public figure is not all glam and glitz.

It sometimes comes with real threats that require a security plan and a skilled close protection team.

The challenge: Client needs exposure, but not to POIs

Our client, a famous celebrity, was experiencing uncomfortable situations in which several admirers were making inappropriate overtures, sending her intimate gifts, and showing up at her residence.

One identified person of interest (POI) appeared at an invitation-only event that the client also attended. We believe he used fake credentials to gain access to the event. As she had an important meeting at the event that she could not reschedule, it was not an option for our client to leave the event.

The solution: Heightened awareness without all the fuss

Because AS Solution's close protection team was aware of the POI prior to the event, they already had plans in place to mitigate any situation.

The team lead suggested that the safest solution would be to leave the venue. But since there was no immediate danger and the POI was identified and under observation, we deferred the decision to the client. She opted to stay for her meeting but agreed to leave as soon as she could thereafter.

Our team kept a close eye on the movements of the POI and our client to ensure their paths did not intersect. The POI's hands and general behavior were closely monitored for any suspicious activity. When the client's meeting concluded, our team had her vehicle waiting in a secure location. Discreetly and without causing a scene, our client was escorted out of the venue.

The results: Just another evening

Our client finished her meeting, maintained her public persona and stayed safe although the POI was at the event. No one was the wiser. Then, we got her out safely.

Success came when our client said, "Thank you", and moved on with her night. She updated her Twitter feed to show off her dress and attended several other social functions that evening.

Turning around an underperforming residential security program

The challenge: Transform a residential security team from underachieving to best-in-class

Our client, the family office of a highly prominent principal in a suburban neighborhood, required an effective residential security program. Risk scenarios ranged from groups of sidewalk gawkers to burglary and home invasion – and clearly identified persons of interest.

The client's former security provider had been lacking in many ways. Despite repeated warnings, the company continued to miss agreed performance targets and the family wasn't happy.

AS Solution was invited to bid on the contract. The only special requests in the RFP were that the new program be as trouble-free for the frustrated family as possible and that "the changing of the guard" present a minimum of disruption.

The solution: Program reboot with built-in quality assurance, team development, and hands-on management

We started with an analysis of the risks facing the principals, then tried to understand the family's preferences concerning residential security. We also interviewed other stakeholders within the residential ecosystem including household staff and managers.

We gained consensus on pain points, expectations and the contours of success to ensure complete transparency in how we would address the issues and arrive at sustainable solutions. There was dissatisfaction with parts but not all of the former setup. Some of the staff were in fact competent and well-liked. The root cause of the dissatisfaction was poor program design and management, not the people doing their shifts.

Our program overhaul introduced standard operating procedures and ongoing quality control including everyday interventions by experienced managers and occasional audits to assess team readiness. We developed KPIs with the family office, then tracked them so we could share performance metrics with the client and agree on corrective action.

Another key part of our program was staff development. We kept on as many of the existing security staff as possible to align with the principal's wishes and minimize disruption during the transition. Our transition plan made clear that staff accountability and ongoing focus on and investment in training and career planning were cornerstones of our HR policy.

The results: Smooth transition to new team management, focus on continual improvement – and a satisfied family

The principal and the family office wanted to do things right rather than do them fast. Still, we know from experience that dragging out such significant changes does no one any good, so we set a target of one month for program redesign and transition – and achieved it.

The new residential security program is currently running smoothly. The best of the former staff – the familiar faces and hands of the program – were retained so the family experienced little uncertainty over new staff and could get on with their lives without thinking more than necessary about residential security.

The program is designed and managed to prevent complacency and future problems. Ongoing quality assurance, staff development, and transparent performance reviews mean the family office has a higher degree of certainty in program viability than previously.

Finally, we were also pleased to have another group of agents that we can use to identify and develop talent. Residential protection positions are important to our own HR efforts, and our managers stay closely involved with them. Many of our best people began their careers in residential protection before moving into management or close protection. So, while such jobs may be end stations in some companies and moonlighting for some agents, for us they are excellent ways to nurture talent and build careers.

Setting up, training and maintaining a covert family security program and surveillance detection program to provide top-notch security

We regularly work with high net worth individuals, families and their offices. In many ways, the protection and security needs of these prominent families are similar to those of corporations. After all, these high net worth individuals are often founders of highly successful companies, and in that sense share many characteristics with the C-suite principals for whom we typically provide executive protection.

In important ways, however, families are not the same as corporations, and neither are their protection needs. Parents would rather their children not notice the added security, as that might make them afraid. Affluent families are first and foremost families and want to do what families do without extra people hovering about nearby. Interestingly, we see the same tendency in more and more corporations, who also are beginning to prefer a more covert protection style for their executives.

The challenge: We were asked to provide a personal protection program for a prominent high net worth individual that integrated work-related executive protection (EP) with 24/7 protection of his family. In addition to the family's prominence, they had also received direct threats.

Our work began with an assessment that identified probable risks (hostile groups and individuals) and then matched these against a vulnerability evaluation of the principal and his family as they moved through their lives.

We then designed a protective program to optimize the family's security and matched it to the family's lifestyle and personal preferences. It was here that this case becomes more than "just another EP program" – but in many ways a typical AS Solution project. The family just wanted to get on with its life as normally as possible and did not want to be encumbered in any way or noticed for its protection. In fact, they required that the EP program basically be invisible to family members as well as the press, colleagues and general public – and still highly effective.

The solution: Based on the probable threats and vulnerabilities discovered in our Risk, Threat, and Vulnerability Analysis (RTVA) process, we created a security master plan including all preventative and emergency procedures. This made for an effective protective program that plugged security vulnerabilities while maintaining the principal's feelings of freedom and privacy – all while being invisible to both the trained and untrained eye.

The solution is based on a combination of covert EP and surveillance detection teams. The covert EP team is tasked with staying "within the bubble", unnoticed by the family and anyone else, and looking out to identify threats as early as possible and to create time and distance between the threat and principals. The surveillance detection team is tasked with staying "outside the bubble", unnoticed by anyone at all, and looking in toward the bubble in order to observe who might be observing the principals – and relaying this information to the EP team as the result of data analysis or in real time; and in the instance of an actual hostile act, intercepting the perpetrators as soon as possible.

Once the tasks were defined, and not before, we helped hire suitable professionals for each specialist role. We even field-tested candidates to assess their integrity, ability to make decisions under pressure, and initiative. Team training has been a critical part of the program's success. After recruitment, the two teams completed two separate, task specific foundation classes on a pass/fail basis.

The results: We are now well into program implementation and are happy to report that we satisfy all principal and shareholder requirements. We have created two small, yet highly specialized, protective details consisting of quality men and women who perform truly covert executive protection and surveillance detection. This results in an effective security system that is unnoticed by the principals and the public eye.

The combination of the covert EP and surveillance detection teams is powerful and gives us a tactical advantage that is exceptionally strong. With traditional overt EP, persons of interest can identify vulnerabilities in our visible protection in order to circumvent it and get to the target; when we combine covert EP with surveillance detection, the perpetrators don't see our protection, and our team can seemingly emerge out of thin air to surprise them and stop attacks earlier and farther away.

Quarterly, we deliver enrichment and refresher training for all team members to sharpen existing skills, add new skills and methods as operations require, and continue their professional development.

Truly personalized residential security is the only kind that really works

Residential security is important to all of us, so it's no wonder that sales of burglar alarms and other home security systems – both monitored and unmonitored – have boomed in recent years.

Unfortunately, many of these systems don't live up to their marketing hype. The reality is that alarms go off for no reason, or don't go off when they should. Call centers don't respond as agreed. Just look at customer service ratings for the largest home security company in the U.S.

The upshot is that homeowners stop using their security systems. Even in Silicon Valley, where median home prices in some zip codes are north of four million dollars, an estimated 90% of homes with security systems simply don't use them. The most common complaints are that they're inconvenient, don't work as expected and are ugly. Sound familiar?

The challenge: Design a home security system that matches the family's lifestyle and that they would be happy to use.

Our client was building a new multi-million-dollar home with a guest annex, and his company required that the new home be equipped with a security system. He couldn't stand using the one installed in his current home, and made it clear to the architects that the new system would have to be all but invisible and work far better than the one he had.

After the architectural team had tried and failed to achieve an acceptable solution with a security system integrator, they called us. Could AS Solution help design a security system for the new home that would meet the client's requirements for a customized system that was also aesthetically pleasing?

The solution: A solid understanding of the family's personal preferences – and close cooperation with architects, contractors and suppliers.

We began by conducting an RTVA, which indicated that home invasion was the most significant risk, even in the upscale neighborhood where the new home was being built.

We then worked with the family to better understand their vision of the ideal security setup and their personal preferences. Where were the pain points of their current system? What were the rhythms of their day and week? How did they like to receive guests? Did they prefer to see who was at the door through a window or via a security camera? What would they do first in case they heard an alarm go off in the middle of the night?

The answers to these and many other questions enabled us to create a security concept that we first tested and refined with the family, then used as our "bible" to work closely with architects, contractors, and suppliers. To strike the right balance between aesthetics, lifestyle, and security, some doors and windows were manufactured according to our specifications, and all security hardware was installed effectively yet unobtrusively.

The result: A customized security system that the family enjoys using

Staying true to the family's lifestyle while respecting architectural ideals and security best practices is only possible through close cooperation, clear communication, and good planning. But when all stakeholders commit to this goal from the start of the building project, rather than taking security on at the end, successful outcomes are much more likely. As was the case here.

The family now has a highly effective security system that is designed around their lifestyle. They and their architects like that it is basically invisible. We like that it is so simple to live with and so aligned with their personal preferences that it actually gets used and serves its purpose: keeping the family safe, happy and productive while at home.

When disaster hits, executive protection goes beyond the C-suite to family and associates

Personal protection is often believed to be a service for C-suite executives, but a quality program can be scaled in a moment's notice to mitigate risks for a principal's family and close associates as well.

The challenge: Devastating wildfire, hurricane-level winds, and a stranded family member

The wife of our client, the CEO of a Fortune 500 company, was staying at a hotel that suddenly came under siege by one of the most destructive wildfires in California's history. The blaze eventually burned 36,810 acres, 2,843 structures, 2,800 homes, and claimed at least 22 lives in California's beautiful wine country.

The Tubbs Fire started around 9:45 pm on Oct. 8, 2017 in Calistoga, California. By 1 am on Oct. 9, the fire had spread to Santa Rosa, where our client's wife was staying at a high-end hotel. Sonoma County officials called for an evacuation of Santa Rosa at 1:30 am.

At 2 am, our Operations Center received a call from our client's security team requesting the evacuation of the CEO's wife. She had left the hotel, leaving her personal belongings behind, and was safe, for the moment, at a friend's house. At the same time, whipped by near hurricane-level winds, flames were now crossing Highway 101, the main roadway in the area.

The solution: 24/7 availability and teamwork

When our operations specialist received the call at 2 am, he alerted his duty manager who relied on his five years of experience and our network to execute the evacuation quickly.

The wildfire's rapid and unpredictable spread required careful coordination between the duty manager, our local partner in the Sonoma County area, and the Fortune 500 company's security team.

The results: A successful ending to a long and frightening night

AS Solution's security driver navigated through smoke-choked roads and rerouted through several detours to arrive at the wife's friend's home by 4 am. She was delivered safely an hour and a half later to the Oakland airport, 70 miles south, where the company jet was waiting to fly her safely home.

By 4:30 am, the winds in the Santa Rosa area reached their peak speed of more than 60 miles per hour. The high-end hotel burned down. The Tubbs Fire was not 100% contained until Oct. 31, 2017.

Staying safe after Hurricane Maria

When Hurricane Maria struck Puerto Rico and other Caribbean islands, it was not just another storm. The category five event was one of most intense hurricanes of all time and came right on the heels of another deadly storm, Hurricane Irma.

Right after the storm, some of our clients with families and homes in Puerto Rico asked us for help in determining their loved ones' wellbeing.

The challenge: Use our local sources to contact stranded family members throughout the island

In the aftermath of the storm, there was no way to get on or off the island, and communication was next to impossible. Once we provided our local partners with the names and addresses of the missing family members, they had the unenviable task of making their way to several cities scattered across the island.

The solution: Record messages of family members so their loved ones know they are safe

After traveling through a badly bruised Puerto Rico, our local sources were able to communicate the condition of our clients' family members via satellite phones. Once some communication lines on the island came back online, our partners sent videos that contained personal messages to our clients from their loved ones. This was crucial as many of the family members lived in remote areas that were offline for considerably longer than the larger cities.

These messages were key because they let our clients assess what was needed for the families. Armed with this knowledge, they were able to create a plan for how to help once resources started flowing to the island. For example, we made sure that some families received power generators and other key supplies as soon as these could be sent.

The results: Fast contact helped make the best of a bad situation

Within 24 hours, we had already contacted many family members. Within a week, we had sent personal video messages from all the Puerto Rican families to their loved ones in the continental United States and around the world.

Our clients were relieved to know that their families were safe and had made it through the storm relatively unscathed.

Don't forget to pack family security for your next family vacation

Corporate travelers are often accustomed to a greater degree of service – including security service – when they are on the road for the company compared to personal vacations.

But as this case illustrates, sometimes just a little bit of travel intelligence and a single security driver can go a long way in keeping everyone safe while enjoying a family holiday.

The challenge: A last-minute trip to Mexico requires a security evaluation

One of our clients decided to travel with his family on a personal trip to Mexico. The destination was a popular tourist hub and typically considered safe. However, the company's security team wanted a security evaluation of the destination prior to departure. The principal and his family were leaving the next day.

The solution: Draw on intelligence from a recent deployment

One of our executive protection teams had just finished escorting a dignitary in the town. Using their network prior to and while on assignment, they became aware of some circumstances that elevated the risk level for travelers in the area.

At the time of travel for the principal and his family, no event had yet occurred, but the risks were still prevalent. We thus recommended that a security driver accompany the family on their vacation. The family agreed to this plan.

The family had a safe vacation and enjoyed their driver. However, shortly after they returned home, the security situation in the town took a turn for the worse, especially for tourists, when several incidents occurred in public areas. A few weeks after the family returned home, there was an attack close to where they had stayed.

The results: A safe trip enabled by timely information

Our team had this insight one month prior to the attack. The U.S. State Department issued a travel risk alert for the area one week after the attack.

When the news reports came in about the attack, the principal called AS Solution to thank us for the excellent suggestion of having a secure driver. His family had a great vacation and felt safe the entire time. They were now aware of how close they could have been to real danger. The principal stated that he will never again make travel plans without advanced security intelligence.

Following a trail: On- and offline breadcrumbs to keep a client safe through intelligence analysis

Handling a potential threat as early and as far away from the principal is the essence of good security. This not only keeps our clients safe; it also gives them the peace of mind they need to get on with their busy lives.

One of the ways that AS Solution mitigates risks at an early stage is our dedicated team of intelligence analysts. Intelligence forms an integral part of strong security programs. It bolsters EP details, supports secure travel services and reinforces residential protection.

In some cases, well-qualified analysts notify agents on the ground of credible threats before they occur, thus preventing emergency situations. In other cases, intel helps to discredit a perceived threat entirely, thus allowing resources to be used more effectively.

The challenge: A prospective client came to us after having received several threats from an unknown source. Could AS Solution find the identity and location of the culprit and take the necessary steps to protect the client?

A prominent high net worth individual came to us after having received several pieces of mail at her home address that threatened family members and herself. She had no idea of who was responsible for the anonymous letters and reached out to us to help identify the perpetrator.

With only the limited amount of information contained in the letters, AS Solution needed to work quickly before the threats escalated.

The solution: Use available information and proven intelligence techniques to identify the person of interest and assess risk

The unhinged person that wrote the letters unwittingly left a few unique indicators that allowed us to ascertain that one individual sent all the letters. By following the clues left in the letters we could create a general profile of this person and determine his location, age, and other valuable information. At that point, we used several open-source intelligence tools and techniques to narrow down the list of potential suspects.

We continued to refine our shortlist until we confirmed the perpetrator's identity. We could then retrieve the suspect's social media profiles to monitor his location. Using only publicly available sources, we were even able to find out that the suspect had been detained by local law enforcement on an unrelated matter in a different part of the country and would be placed under house arrest. By digitally tracing his footsteps and whereabouts, we determined that he would be unlikely to carry out his threats.

The results: AS Solution notified the client of our findings and ensured her that she was at no immediate risk

Upon discovering that she and her family no longer had to worry about the individual, our client could relax and go back to her normal daily routines.

The client was so pleased with how we resolved the issue that she has reached out to us on several occasions since then to conduct similar intelligence gathering.

A sudden explosion on client's evening stroll route? A walk in the park for a protective team connected to an efficient command center

Providing effective protective security without wrapping the client within a claustrophobic bubble is inherently difficult. You need to be prepared for anything and everything – usually with little to no warning – and at the same time enable clients to get on with their lives without feeling encumbered by ever-present protection teams.

A cornerstone of the AS Solution approach is our ongoing dedication to adapting our services to the client's personal preferences and corporate culture. Flexibility is key, but so is unswerving devotion to risk mitigation. Balancing these competing demands is what keeps our clients safe without being inconvenienced.

The challenge: Let the client get on with his daily routine despite potential risks due to a worrisome local incident

Our client, a high net worth individual that frequently travels for business, was staying in New York City for a series of special events. After another long day of meetings, negotiations and public appearances, the client liked to go for a casual walk through the neighborhood to clear his mind and prepare for the next day's activities.

While such a stroll does pose some security concerns, this is usually not a difficult task for our protective team. However, on this particular evening personnel at AS Solution Operations Center (ASOC) became aware of reports of an explosion in the neighborhood where our client likes to take his walk.

How could AS Solution keep the principal safe without disrupting his beloved routine?

The solution: Use our intelligence capabilities to convey important information to the security team before they enter a high-risk area – and enable them to redirect the principal's route

The team at our command center discovered multiple reports of an explosion near the principal's hotel before the story was picked up by the media. Remembering the client's predilection for an evening walk and realizing that our protective team in New York had no way of knowing what had occurred just moments earlier, the ASOC team immediately contacted the NYC team to convey all available information regarding the incident.

As it turns out this occurred precisely when our team and principal were proceeding to the lobby of the hotel. Our agents shared the information with the principal and recommended alternative plans for how to proceed.

The results: Another relaxing walk despite a lot of local commotion

The client weighed his options and decided to take his cherished walk, but to follow the suggested detour and avoid the usual area. He enjoyed yet another leisurely stroll at the end of another eventful day – without being disturbed by the commotion of sirens and the hordes of on-lookers.

Intelligence gathered by our ASOC team, transferred across the country in seconds to our on-the-ground team, enabled the client to make an informed decision – and get on with his life.

Creating a more culturally aware team: How AS Solution makes our global clients feel at ease

The ability to operate worldwide is one of the many ways we help our clients to achieve their business objectives. But what makes us a truly global company is the diversity of our staff and clientele. In addition to serving American businesses that operate at home and abroad, we also work for entrepreneurs, high net worth individuals and corporations from around the world.

Whether on a security detail in a foreign country or at the corporate campus of a Fortune 500 company, we are routinely involved in dealing with many people from different cultural backgrounds. As even the smallest point of disconnect can lead to a security lapse or a moment of embarrassment for the principal, we go to great lengths to ensure that our clients are comfortable with their protective team. Sometimes establishing this level of comfort requires our team to learn new tasks...or even 16th century Japanese history.

The challenge: Familiarize a residential protection team with the cultural etiquette of a new principal and his family

Our client was a Japanese expat that frequently receives colleagues and guests from his home country. Due to the stature of his guests and frequent contact between them and the protection team, we wanted our client to be assured that the nuances of Japanese etiquette would not be overlooked.

Could AS Solution find a way to bridge the cultural divide between the security team and the principal?

The solution: Use AS Solution's industry-leading internal training division to create a course on Japanese cultural etiquette

Thanks to our new training division, we can offer tailor made and customizable courses for practically anything our staff or clients request. While courses are usually related to protective security topics such as enhanced intelligence gathering techniques or a crash course on covert surveillance, this presented a great opportunity to expand our scope and provide a new type of service for our team.

After a careful examination of Japanese cultural components, business practices and even a touch of political and historical information, we made a course that helped our team gain a better understanding and a deeper appreciation of our client's cultural background. The course was then shared with staff members who participated virtually and gave their feedback.

The results: The course was a success. Our staff enjoyed learning about a new topic, the client and his family appreciated our effort, and we could provide smoother security at the principal's residence

Armed with additional cultural background information, our team was able to provide a better and more personalized service for the principal. The client was impressed at our team's level of commitment and was genuinely appreciative that they took the time to learn about his culture. This has strengthened the security process in several ways. The team gained expertise that helped them meet the principal's cultural expectations, and how to facilitate a smoother screening process with friends, acquaintances and other guests coming to the home.

The ability to implement such courses requires two things: experience in developing and distributing tailor-made course materials, and dedicated staff that is eager to learn. AS Solution is fortunate to have both.